For many Afrikans true freedom may only unveil itself in death. We are held back from accomplishing our dreams in many ways. We are hindered at every step, every doorway. It is not enough for a few of us to advance, this will lead to seperation, as a few sheep in the wilderness are easily trapped and lost. As a people we must pull together, to fight not just a people, but an idea. The key is to help and be helped.

Sadly our greatest enemy is ourselves.

I hope you achieve everything you are striving for. But I'm sure you will. Confidence is the right pathway to take.

Love Mich
xxx
x

Life on
Death Row

"If you have no confidence in self you are twice defeated in the race of life. With confidence you have won even before you have started."

Marcus Garvey.

Life on Death Row

One man's fight against racism
and the death penalty

Merrilyn Thomas

PIATKUS

Acknowledgements

I would like to thank the very many people who have given me help and support during the writing of this book. To name them all would take several pages, but in particular I would like to mention Clive Stafford Smith, without whom the book would not have been possible; Paul Hamann for allowing me to make use of some of his unique photographs; Jan Arriens for sharing with me something of his personal relationship with Sam Johnson; my colleagues at work in the Cambridge Weekly News office, especially my editor Colin Moule and news editor Sue Elliott, who gave me the necessary backing and put up with my frequent absences with equanimity; my schoolfriend Gill Cormode of Piatkus Books, whose sensitive support and guidance has helped to bring this book to fruition and whose friendship, which now encompasses that of editor and author, is all the more valued for that extra dimension; Henry Hudson and his wife Mary Beth in Mississipi, who offered me the hospitality of their home and provided me with an oasis of sanity in an insane world; and finally, but most importantly, my family – David, who gave me the encouragement to start on the project and keep going, and my children, Megan and Morag, who accepted, sometimes reluctantly, my role as absentee mother.

© 1989 Merrilyn Thomas

First published in 1989 by
Judy Piatkus (Publishers) Ltd,
5 Windmill Street, London W1P 1HF

British Library Cataloguing in Publication Data
Thomas, Merrilyn
   Life on death row : one man's fight against racism
   and the death penalty.
   1. United States. Condemned prisoners
   I. Title
   365'.4'0973

   ISBN 0-86188-879-0

Photograph of Clive Stafford Smith courtesy of the
Cambridge Evening News. Other photographs kindly
supplied by Paul Hamann and the author.

"There's a Tear in my Beer" words and music by
Hank Williams © Acuff Rose Music Inc.
Lyrics reproduced by permission of Acuff Rose/
Opryland Music Ltd.

Phototypeset in 11/12½ pt Compugraphic Plantin by
Action Typesetting Ltd., Gloucester
Printed and bound in Great Britain by
Billing & Sons Ltd, Worcester

This book is dedicated to my mother, Winifred Thomas, who gave up her own struggle for life during the writing of it. For five and a half years she was a prisoner of a different kind, paralysed and almost without speech after a severe stroke. But throughout it all, until the end, she maintained her love of life and her will to live. She too was an example of the strength and courage that can sustain those faced with the direst circumstances.

Contents

Foreword

by Clive A. Stafford Smith

Yesterday, the State of Mississippi, in the United States of America, executed Leo Edwards. Somewhere between the reality of today and yesterday, the State of Mississippi played God and took Leo Edwards' life in the gas chamber at Parchman Penitentiary. It happened right in front of me, as I sat helpless, unable to save him or even comfort him. First Edward Earl Johnson, and now Leo. How many more?

In *Life on Death Row*, Merrilyn Thomas writes of the life and death of Edward Earl Johnson, killed by cyanide gas on May 20th 1987. I represented Edward for the last three weeks of his life, in an effort to stave off that final tragedy. I had known him for several years, as one of the 48 men and women on Mississippi Death Row. He was quite a man and not a day goes by without my thinking of him.

I am going to leave his story and my involvement in it to Merrilyn, who shares my memories of Edward.

When Merrilyn asked me to write a foreword to the book, I said I would when I could. I work for the Southern Prisoners' Defense Committee and I had just heard that Leo Edwards had been scheduled for execution on June 21st 1989 – yesterday now, but back then I had 28 days in which to secure a stay. Writing a foreword was far from my mind, but today it may act as a catharsis.

Leo was 37 when he died. He was brought up in New Orleans, in a 'proud but poor' family. Leo's father developed a tumour in the head, and turned to drink and to abusing the family. At the age of twelve, Leo was introduced to another man who introduced him gradually, through the stages of addiction, to beer, marijuana and heroin. Leo graduated from spending his pocket money to spending the proceeds of petty theft on his physical cravings. He was being trained to squander not only money and health, but any chance that he may have had to develop his soft-spoken, philosophical soul along the channels approved by society.

In 1980, Leo went to Mississippi, where he met Mikel White. The two of them shared the habit, both lost to the normal world in the day-in, day-out ritual of shooting up. Together, they committed three armed robberies

1

to finance their needs, and three *Stop'n'Go* store clerks lay dead. Three tragedies for three families, all for less money than would keep Leo's withdrawal symptoms at bay for a week. The prosecution could make out no apparent reason why the clerks had to die, once the money had been handed over.

When Merrilyn writes of Edward's death in *Life on Death Row*, she is dealing with a clear-cut case against capital punishment. Edward had no prior convictions, was only eighteen when he was arrested, and was − to my subjective certainty − not even guilty of the crime charged. Leo, in contrast, had half a dozen prior offences, was already 27 and was, in all probability, present at the scene of three crimes of murder. Some would say, without taking the time to learn who Leo was, that Leo was an archetypal example of a criminal for whom death should be the only punishment.

Leo's life and execution were, indeed, archetypal of those on Death Row, USA.

Leo was black, he was tried in Hinds County, Mississippi, where the population is 40 percent black. As in every capital case, the prosecutor, Ed Peters, was allowed to strike twelve jurors from the jury and, as in every case, he removed black people.

Peters did not seek death against Mikel White, because a few days before, when White's trial had begun, Peters had been unable to secure the kind of jury he preferred − all white, all pro-death penalty. Instead, Peters made a deal with White, for a life sentence in exchange for his testimony against Leo. Only after the deal was struck did Peters learn that White had been recognised by the victim in the robbery. Leo, who was from out of town, had not been recognised. The obvious inference was that the clerk had to die, or White would be identified. Only one gun was involved, and there was strong evidence in support of Leo's testimony that he had not fired the fatal shots, nor intended that anyone should be killed.

But by that time, the die had been cast.

Leo told me last week, 'When I saw the jury, I thought, "I'm dead".' True enough. Two days later, those twelve white people sentenced Leo to be gassed. Mikel White was given a life sentence and will shortly be eligible for parole.

Leo took his first appeal to the Mississippi Supreme Court, and then sought review from the Supreme Court of the United States. Two years after he was sentenced to die, Leo was back before the state court seeking a writ of error *coram nobis*, a quaint antiquated name for the next layer of appellate review. The eight year appellate process which would end in Leo's death was well under way.

Meanwhile, it was with a brash honesty that District Attorney Peters answered a reporter's questioning on his 'philosophy' when seeking the death penalty: When he was picking a jury, he said he just tried to 'get rid of as many blacks as possible.'

We all *know* that is the way it is, but no prosecutor has had the gall to admit it so brazenly since lynching and the Ku Klux Klan began to slip out of vogue. But Peters said it again, on television. And again in court when subpoenaed by Ken Rose, who was then Leo's attorney. And had Peters applied his 'philosophy' in Leo's case? An unqualified 'Yes'.

By this time – 1985 – the United States was well into the Reagan 'Revolution', which in the opinion of many sought to legitimize the rich getting richer and the poor getting forgotten. But surely even the Supreme Court would not stand for racial discrimination of this kind. Indeed, in 1986 the Court specifically decided that jurors could not be excluded on the basis of their skin colour in *Batson v. Kentucky*. Racial discrimination was condemned as 'odious in all respects'.

However, court after court turned Leo down. The Mississippi Supreme Court denied *coram nobis* relief. The Federal District Court in Hinds County denied *habeas corpus*, another Latin term which once guaranteed the black defendant a fair shake in the South. *Batson*, it was held, should not be applied 'retroactively', since Peters was not 'on notice' at the time of trial that he should not discriminate! The Federal Circuit Court affirmed. Then, in the most crushing blow of all, the Supreme Court again denied review in early 1989.

I had known Leo for several years and had worked closely with Ken Rose, Leo's appellate lawyer, on many cases. I had promised both of them that I would help out. Perhaps we could seek further appeals or file what is known as a 'successor' *habeas corpus* petition.

It was with a heavy heart, though, that I reviewed the case. The Federal Courts in Mississippi have been overwhelmed by conservative judges appointed by Ronald Reagan, and nobody has succesfully secured a stay of execution on a successor petition for several years. Indeed, the new philosophy of the *laissez-faire* Reagan years permits the execution of minor accomplices when the triggerman goes free. It permits the execution of the retarded, and even of children. In Edward Johnson's case, the Federal Appeals Court had actually criticised me for 'wasting' their time with further appeals. As 108 men, one woman, and two children have died these past few years, some of us have come to know when heartless judges will grow impatient. Leo did not really know it, but he was as good as dead.

But what else can one do? Leo had less than a month of life remaining, and hope was all that would help him through those terrible 28 days. If he had no hope, he would have nothing to distract him from simple arithmetic – he would be dead in just 40,000 minutes – and nothing to prevent him from watching in agony as each minute slipped by.

So I drowned my sadness in more than 100 hours' labour each week, and tried to distract Leo's agony with over 1,000 pages of petitions, filed at every level of state and federal courts in the country. His successor petition in Federal Court was filed on the 3,000th day Leo had spent waiting to die.

Trying to find a new angle, I even filed a complaint with the Inter-American Commission on Human Rights setting out the facts of the discrimination. The Commission indicated that Leo's complaint had merit and asked Mississippi to stay the execution, but the request was ignored.

The final denial from the courts came just hours before the time set for his execution. Leo died on that 3,008th day. On the tip of my right middle finger, I can still feel the texture of his skin where I touched him on the shoulder, as I said goodbye. It was 10.00 pm, two hours before the midnight hour. An hour before, I had taken his weeping wife, Janice, over to Parchman's 'Spiritual Life Centre'. She had collapsed, screaming, when the guards told her she had to leave, and I had to half-carry her out to the waiting van.

Two years ago, when 'they' killed Edward Earl Johnson, I had been allowed to stay until the moment Edward had been closed into the gas chamber. Surely nobody should be denied a friend in those final, terrible hours. But the new prison governor had come up with his new battery of emotion-erasing regulations, and lawyers had to leave at 9.30. I am not above begging, but even that could only produce permission to stay until ten.

My God, if there were not enough decency in Leo to talk of other things, I could speak for hours on the courage of the man. What would *you* say if you were saying 'goodbye', knowing that two hours later you would be choking to death in the gas chamber? He sat there, calm as can be, giving me his last messages: Break the news gently to his mother, Helen, with a doctor standing by, for she was on oxygen, recently hospitalised for heart problems. Tell Janice, his wife, that he loved her. Tell his fifteen-year-old daughter, Lataresha, to be strong, and to work to get into university.

For me, just two requests: First, to help Lataresha get into Georgetown University if I could, since that was her dream. Second, to be sure that he would be buried in New Orleans, near his family, and that the prison did not just 'dump my corpse'. When the guard told me I had to leave, Leo looked up and smiled, and told me to listen to a song called 'The Skin I'm In' by The Cameos. That would help me understand what it meant to be black and be in his predicament. Finally, he told me to 'keep the faith', because a lot of the others there on Death Row still needed help.

Ken and I came back two hours later, after gently breaking the inevitability of Leo's death to his family. Ken and I had to come back to watch and listen as Leo gasped for life.

Leo, and his final days, tell much of the story of the death penalty in the United States. It is a story or arbitrariness and caprice. It is a story of prison officials' desperate attempt to create the illusion that an execution is just part of the job, rather than a very human, and inhumane, event. It is the sad story of how many people who never met Leo, and whose only knowledge of him was a criminal record, thought that he was the incarnation of unmitigated evil.

As I reflect on what was, and what might have been, it is frustrating to recognise the other seemingly immutable rules which contribute to the execution of a person such as Leo.

1. Capital Punishment: When those without the capital get the punishment

To be poor is to have the unique privilege of an appointment with the executioner. While the lightning bolt of electrocution strikes at random, one time in a thousand, among those accused of murder in the United States everyone executed shares the badge of poverty.

It is a simple matter of getting what you pay for, and the poor have no access to the flashy and effective lawyers who defend Oliver North or John DeLorean. Leo would have told you about one of his neighbours on Death Row who was represented by a law *student*. Her first words to the Judge were, 'May I have a moment to compose myself, Your Honour? I have never been in a courtroom before.' Thus, although the death penalty is theoretically available only in cases of murder, one of my black clients in Mississippi received the ultimate punishment from an all-white jury for statutory rape.

Another of Leo's neighbours was represented by a lawyer who admitted to drinking vodka during the trial, and who clipped handcuffs on himself without checking to see if anyone had the key. He spent the rest of the trial in shackles, and his client now spends his time on Death Row. Another lawyer referred to his own client as a 'nigger' when addressing the (all-white) jury.

Nobody with the means to pay for an effective defence *ever* ends up on Death Row in the United States of America. However, what happens to the poor person once on Death Row is more disturbing still. The Supreme Court recently decided that someone sentenced to die has absolutely no constitutional right to state-funded counsel for the ten or more levels of appeal after trial and direct appeal. Thus, a mentally retarded person who cannot write his or her own name, or a child who has been sentenced to death, is meant to research and litigate in this most complicated field of law. We have surely stepped through the Looking Glass.

One quarter of those on Death Row are retarded, and the Supreme Court recently said that it is permissible to execute those with the mental age of a six-year-old. Some are children, ranging from the youngest (one of my clients, Troy Dugar, who was fifteen at the time of the crime, and was sentenced to die on his sixteenth birthday) on up to the ripe old age of seventeen.

Many more on Death Row suffer from severe mental illnesses. 'Justice' – being blind – supposes that these people can represent themselves in the intensely complex field of capital litigation.

If not represented by someone who is willing to do it without payment, then these poor folk are likely to end up without representation at all. Troy Dugar would not care, since he suffers on Death Row as a juvenile, has a mental age of nine or ten, and the experience of eight years of schizophrenic delusions behind him. He does not even understand that he is on Death Row.

2. Plus ça change, plus c'est la même chose?

Somehow, a system which picks so concertedly upon the poor, the black and the disenfranchised provokes a series of remarkable coincidences to advertise its own inequity. Two of my clients, one from Georgia and one from Alabama, caused me great confusion. Both had an IQ of 49, getting fewer answers right than a friend's two-and-a-half year-old daughter; both flunked the competency test used in England in the time of Henry VIII;

both 'confessed' under my questioning to assassinating President Kennedy; neither knew whether he was Chinese; and both were named Jerome Holloway.

As Leo watched his appeals unfold, he would have been the first to tell you that the Death Penalty is an eternal saga of truth is stranger than fiction. By the end, Leo was shell-shocked by more than eight years of one paradox after another, all of which apparently went unnoticed by the revengeful viewing audience.

Leo's execution, by pure happenstance, was set for the 25th anniversary of the Ku Klux Klan's murder of the three Civil Rights workers in Philadelphia, Mississippi, on June 21st 1964. This event was subsequently dramatised in the film *Mississippi Burning*.

On June 21 1989, Governor Ray Mabus was scheduled to give a speech in Philadelphia on the 'New Mississippi', where KKK lynchings were to be relegated to an embarrassing chapter of the State's history, and where the 'Politics of Race' were banished for once and for all. A few hours before this speech, Mabus was to have the final say on whether Leo Edwards would live or die.

Four hours before midnight, after refusing even to meet the man whose fate he was to decide, Governor Mabus said that Leo should die.

It is profoundly depressing when the politics of hypocrisy win out over the politics of decency. But perhaps, in certain ways, Mississippi really *has* changed. Although their wishes were ignored, 100 black elected officials petitioned Mabus to stay the execution – and 25 years ago there were no black elected officials. Just as slow change may come even in Mississippi's race relations, Leo would have told you that, inevitably, slow change will lead us away from the death penalty. But that is small comfort for Leo Edwards and Edward Earl Johnson.

3. Life on Death Row: For those forgotten by the world

I have already lost the battle to save Edward's and Leo's lives. While in the overwhelming majority of cases we are able to preclude the death penalty, in occasional cases it will be Ronald Reagan's legacy that I will lose other legal battles to save lives. I know this to be true, but it is difficult to face up to the fact that two or three of the 38 people I now represent will walk into that execution chamber. I know of no tragedy quite like it.

Watching the news, it is natural that we should all feel sorry for the students crushed in Tiananman Square, 'executed' by the mindless octogenarians of the Chinese hierarchy. We all feel sorry for those tortured and killed in Chile, Argentina or Paraguay by the totalitarian dictators of recent decades. We all feel sorry for these victims, and I suppose it is of some comfort to the victims of repression and torture that they have supporters inside and outside their own countries, and that often the torturer feels constrained to conduct the gruesome business in secrecy.

Because these other victims receive almost universal sympathy, I sometimes think that those on Death Row suffer the harshest fate of all. It is not just the 3,000 days of waiting to die in a solitary cell. It is not just the periodic failures of the electric chair as when, for example, the poor, retarded Horace Dunkins was taken out of the thing while it was fixed, and then tortured to death with 2,000 volts coursing between his shaved head and his right ankle for several minutes.

I happened to notice today that there are currently 2,186 men, women and children on Death Row in the United States, with more being added almost every day. At current rates, if we execute one person a day, every day but Sunday, for the next ten years, there will still be over 2,000 people waiting to be killed. The numbers are horrifying, but they are also largely ignored. The people on Death Row are generally totally forgotten by the world and, when they are not forgotten, they must suffer the indignity of reading in the press that they are disgusting animals without any redeeming virtues.

It is very hard to listen to people – whom you have never met, and who know nothing about you – opine that you are unmitigated *scum*, day-in, day-out, for 3,000 days. It is very difficult to do what Edward Earl Johnson was forced to do: watch the news on television while a poll is conducted on whether he should die. Some people say no, but most say yes. They used to turn their thumbs up, or down, in the Roman amphitheatres, and one can only imagine the terrified fascination with which the vanquished gladiator watched those audiences 2,000 years ago.

As Edward illustrates so well, often Society's presumption that those on Death Row are scum should, rightfully, be dissolved by the fact that the person is innocent. Joe O'Dell is still on Death Row in Virginia, although someone else has confessed to the crime.

On another level, however, without deprecating the immense tragedy suffered by the victims of crime, the simple fact is that Leo Edwards was not 'scum' – far from it. If we were all judged solely on the basis of the worst act we had ever committed, none of us would look very good.

Whatever Leo's involvement in the sad crime that took human life, those who judged him on one dimension as a result of that fact were wrong, very wrong.

However, because of stereotype, and because most of them come from tragically fragmented families, these very human Human Beings on Death Row often have *no* friends. When I first met Johnny Mack Westbrook, he had not seen anybody from outside Georgia's Death Row for six years. Since he is retarded, nobody bothered to write to him.

It is for this reason that it was so very heartening to Leo, as it has been to me, to see people around the world taking such a human interest in those waiting to die in the United States, lending such support to the helpless. In those final days, Leo showed me letters from England, the Netherlands, Australia and Canada, all wishing him well. I was able to tell him of the demonstration outside the American Embassy in Oslo, demanding justice on his behalf.

Most heartening of all, perhaps, have been the ties that have bound Cambridge in England to these men and women on Death Row. I was born in Addenbrookes Hospital in Cambridge, as was Nicholas Ingram, who now waits on Death Row in Georgia. The link to Cambridge, however, is now much stronger than Nick and me. Merrilyn Thomas has written this book, doing much to bring the injustice of Edward Earl Johnson's death into continuing focus. Jan Arriens, working out of Whittlesford, is coordinating over 100 Englishmen and women who are corresponding with people on Death Row, giving just that human touch which has been lacking for so long.

Words simply cannot express what it is like to wait and watch while Society takes measured steps towards killing someone you love, in what can only be described as a primitive ritual. There is nothing which can erase the disgust I feel when I recall those moments.

However, neither can anything take away treasured moments, such as Leo's reunification with his daughter, Lateresha. Leo had not seen her for eight years, and I spent almost as much time, energy and money tracking her down as I did litigating his case. When I saw the two of them together, and when Leo smiled at me over her shoulder, *everything* was worthwhile.

Clive A. Stafford Smith
June 1989

One
The Execution

The young Englishman sat hunched at the back of the room, his head bowed, eyes tightly shut. Even so he held his hands over his face, as though fearing that he would see what he could not bear to see.

A few yards away from him, in the execution chamber, the black man, his friend, was dying. Dying for a crime he swore he did not commit. Clive did not see. But he could not block out the sounds of death. The desperate gasping for breath as the poisonous cyanide gas filled the airtight chamber where the black man sat, strapped to the chair. Nor could he ignore the excited chatter of the others who had gathered to watch the bizarre spectacle. Ghouls, Clive called them, and waves of nausea hit him.

The Mississippi night air was damp and heavy outside the execution block of the state penitentiary. Clive, in his rumpled, open-necked shirt, could feel the sweat dripping down his back. One of the guards had turned off the air conditioning in the small room where the group was gathered to witness the final minutes in the life of the 26-year-old prisoner. Clive had almost refused to take part in this last macabre ritual. But his sense of duty towards the black man, his loyalty, his friendship, had forced him to be there. He had failed him in his attempts to stop the ghastly procedure. He could not fail him now.

*　　　*　　　*

The last chapter in the life of the man now strapped into the chair in the gas chamber had begun a mere 50 minutes earlier. It was then that Clive Stafford Smith, American attorney at law, had received the news by telephone from his colleague that his final attempt to win a reprieve for his client had been unsuccessful. 'The Governor denied,' Clive's colleague had said. Only three words, but three words that signalled the end. The

11

Governor of the State of Mississippi had decided not to show clemency.

There was little change in the expression on Clive's already tired and drawn face as the words – so expected, so harsh – entered his mind and heart. And yet, for him, it was the hardest moment of his life. There had been little in his 27 years to prepare him for this agonising moment. His roots lay in another world, thousands of miles away in the English countryside with his prosperous Cambridgeshire family. A burning ideal had brought him to this prison in the American Deep South to mix with murderers and executioners – a passionate dedication to the abolition of the death penalty. Tonight, for the first time, he faced the reality.

His lawyer's mind had held out no great hope of a reprieve. The Governor had not acquired a reputation for mercy in his years in office. But Clive had not allowed himself to think beyond this point in the three weeks he had spent fighting a desperate legal battle to save the life of Edward Earl Johnson. Now he had to face the fact that it was all but over. For a moment he continued to sit in the small, bare prison office. In his cell, a stone's throw away, Edward was likewise sitting, waiting. Clive knew he must go to him, and yet he could not go. How could he tell him that it had been decreed that he should die?

He sat for a minute that stretched into eternity, frozen in mind and body. Then, from somewhere, the thought came to him. How could he be so selfish? How could he sit there thinking of his own anguish when Edward was about to die? Clive stood up and left the room. Four locked doors stood between him and Edward. As he approached each one a guard stepped forward and unlocked it. No words were necessary. None was said.

He entered the Death Row gallery with slow, aching steps. To reach Edward's cell he must pass the barred cells of the thirteen other condemned men on the same gallery, all of them dying a little more that night, dying with Edward. Their eyes were upon him. Clive straightened his shoulders and raised his bowed head. He must not let them see his hopelessness, his dejection.

He quickened his pace down the corridor and entered the cell where Edward sat on the narrow bunk. Beside him sat a young woman, Edward's minister. Clive slowly sat down on the bed beside Edward and placed his arm around the black man's shoulder. 'He turned us down,' he told him. Edward did not reply. He seemed totally unmoved. There was nothing to be said. Nothing at all.

Sandy, the minister, suggested praying. She was young and white and preached God's message in the simple manner of a child. It meant little to Clive, but he was glad of her presence. There was a purpose in everything

God did, she said. Clive drew little comfort from her words. He did not wish to be told that God had a purpose for this senseless barbarism. He did not know if her words helped Edward, but could only hope they did. Clive could think of nothing other than to tell Edward that he loved him, that many, many people loved him. Edward looked straight ahead. 'It's strange,' he said in his gentle manner, 'but I feel absolutely no fear.' He was so young, so calm. 'Yes,' he politely agreed with Sandy. 'There is still time for a miracle.'

The three continued to sit on the bed in the dimly lit cell. All around were silent. It was as though they were cocooned in a strange time warp. The minutes went so slowly – and yet they were the last minutes of Edward's life and they were going by so fast. There was a strange feeling of having to do something, say something to pass the time, as though at a bad party. But nobody wanted the time to pass.

Forty minutes to go. Only ten had passed since Clive had heard that there was to be no miracle, whatever Sandy or Edward believed. Cabana, the warden in charge of the prison and of this night's execution, came into the cell. A thick-set man with a bull neck, his brutish appearance belied a more reflective character. He looked what he was, a veteran of Vietnam with years of prison service behind him. But on this night his bond was with the man he was soon to kill. Like hijackers with their victims, he was a part of the team. Together the four of them had no past and no future. They were alone and they had to go through it together. Only for Edward there was to be no getting through.

Cabana had come to tell him they must move to another cell. The rules of the ritual required it. At this time, some faceless bureaucrat had decreed, they must move out of the Death Row cell to the isolation cell, only a few yards away but a few yards nearer to the gas chamber. The logic of the move escaped Clive, other than to increase the torture of the wait. It was death by degrees.

The three rose and followed the guards. The isolation cell was a small whitewashed room with two heavy, solid steel doors, one leading in from Death Row and the other leading out to the gas chamber. There was a tiny window above a prayer bench and a simple wooden cross made by a fellow prisoner. Clive, Edward and Sandy seated themselves on the bench again, the closeness of their bodies being the only way they knew to bring comfort and strength to each other.

Edward continued to talk of hope as though trying to raise the spirits of the others. Sandy read again from the Bible. Clive could say nothing. The expression on his face had become fixed. He held Edward's hand tightly in his own. There was nothing appropriate that could be said. Cabana broke the silence. 'Edward,' he said. 'I have to tell you that I have a tremendous respect for you. And you'll remember what you promised me. You'll put in a good word for me with the Man Upstairs.' His words were so crass, so jarring. But he was trying, in the only way he knew how, to ease the torment of these minutes. He could not be blamed for his clumsiness. He was faced with the impossible task of being kind to a man he was going to kill. Clive almost felt sorry for him.

He searched his mind for a way of breaking the agonising silence that followed Cabana's speech. Turning to Edward, he managed to smile. 'It ain't over till it's over,' he said. It was a baseball expression they had used before, a sort of shorthand between them. Edward responded with a squeeze of the hand. Clive felt Edward was trying to help the others in the room as much as they were trying to help him. He could feel a strange ebb and flow of hope, coupled with the need to prepare for the inevitable.

Another age had gone by and there were 30 minutes to go until midnight – the appointed hour. Would they find it harder to carry out this evil ritual in broad daylight, wondered Clive. Cabana spoke again. It seemed as though he considered it his duty as a human being to explain to the condemned man exactly what was going to happen to him. Was the fear of the unknown greater than the fear of the known? 'I'm going to tell you this so you won't be surprised by anything,' he said to Edward. 'In a few minutes two medical personnel will come in and they will tape two stethoscopes to your chest. They'll also tape two ECG terminals to you. They may have to shave a little hair off to do that. They'll put them on so that they can tell when your heart stops beating. OK? I just want you to know what they are doing.'

Edward nodded like a child in a dental chair who had just been told that the dentist was going to drill a little hole and he wouldn't feel anything at all. The thought wandered unbidden into Clive's mind that the Nazi method of telling their concentration camp victims that a shower awaited them in the gas chamber was better than this. It was all so unreal. Edward sitting there so calmly, nodding as Cabana spoke, and he and Sandy just listening as if this was really something quite normal for civilised people to do. He was having trouble convincing himself that it really was happening. He kept waiting for someone to say that the play acting could stop, they could all go home now. And then Clive would get up and leave and take Edward with him back to his home and his wife in Atlanta where reality was.

But it did not stop. Soon the medics would come, as Cabana had said they would, and Edward would be wired up for his death. Edward spoke, shattering Clive's illusion. 'Mr Cabana,' he said, turning to the prison officer, 'I just want to thank you for everything you've done for me.' Clive could hardly believe that he had heard aright. In his head he could hear the echoes of his mother's voice talking to him as a child back in England: 'Never leave a party without saying thank you.' Then Edward turned to Sandy. 'You've done a lot for me these days, but I want you to remember that you've got a lot more to do out there,' he said, pointing to where the other 45 men on Death Row lay on their bunks. 'Don't ever give up. You've got to remember that. Don't ever give up. And tell my family not to take it too hard, OK?'

Clive sat there, afraid of what Edward might say to him. He had tried, goodness knows, he had tried. But he could not help reproaching himself for failing to win a reprieve. There were all the 'if onlys'. If only he had taken the case earlier. But he had been called in by the family a mere three weeks ago at the last minute, in an eleventh-hour attempt to prevent the execution. What can anyone do in three weeks after seven years of legal manoeuvres? If only he had believed, as he did now, that Edward was innocent of the crime for which he was about to die. He had not killed the white policeman that night in Walnut Grove, Mississippi. But three weeks before Clive had not known that. Edward was just another of his Death Row cases, although one with a degree of urgency that others did not have. He had gone into it with an open mind, neither believing nor disbelieving Edward's protestations of innocence. Gradually, as he examined the evidence, went over the transcripts of the original trial and subsequent appeals and saw where Edward's previous lawyers had failed him through ignorance and inexperience, got to know the man now sitting beside him, played chess with him and talked to him, he knew, with an absolute certainty, that this man was not a murderer. Why, even some of the guards on Death Row agreed he did not do it. But Clive had not known this three weeks before. He had decided to fight the case on legal technicalities. Twenty-one days was not long enough in which to decide the question of innocence or guilt, even if the courts had let him raise it as an issue. So he had fought the case on procedural issues – and lost. Would it have made any difference if he had tried to prove Edward's innocence from the start? The question would always be there. He would never know the answer.

In a fair world Clive knew he would have won the case easily. But it is not a fair world. Was there something he could have done that he did not do? There is always something. And so Clive looked at Edward and knew that he had failed him and was afraid.

Edward turned to him. 'Thank you, Clive,' he said. 'You have done everything you could have done.' He smiled. 'It ain't over till it's over,' he said. The tears welled into Clive's eyes but he managed to fight them back before Edward saw them. He could not break down now – for Edward's sake.

Then again there was the silence. The room was hot and oppressive. Clive fanned the air with a legal pad. He was thankful when Sandy suggested singing something and pointed to a verse in the Bible. Neither he nor Edward knew the tune but they joined in anyway. It was somehow strengthening to hear voices, even if out of tune. Cabana stood silently by, but at times his lips moved as though he too were joining in.

Afterwards they sat together for a while, Clive with his arm tightly around Edward's shoulder, while Sandy gripped his hand. Unprompted Edward spoke again. 'I suppose everyone wonders what a man thinks when he is about to die,' he said. It was a question thrown out, without an answer. 'Well, it ain't over till it's over.'

Then the medics came in and told Edward to lift up his shirt. Clive was glad Edward did not look at him then. He was filled with anger and shame. The men took some heavy grey binding tape such as that used to secure a parcel and wrapped it tightly around Edward's chest. Edward helped them, politely holding it in place for them. One of them shaved a little hair from each shoulder and attached the electrocardiograph contacts. Soon these would be connected up to the monitor outside the gas chamber, the trace would go flat and Edward would be officially dead. They left nothing to chance, these people.

The men left. Edward sat there, naked from the waist up, wearing the indicators of death. It was Sandy who gently told him to replace his shirt, restoring a little of his dignity after this horrible scene. 'It's rather tight. Perhaps they want to suffocate me already,' was all he said.

Now it was almost midnight. 'It's time,' said Cabana. Edward reached over and hugged Sandy. Then, child-like, he kissed her on her cheek and said goodbye. Next he turned to Clive, ready to say his farewell to him too. 'No,' said Clive. 'I'm coming with you.'

And so they walked together down the corridor towards the gas chamber, the tall, gangly young lawyer and the condemned black man, an arm around each other's shoulders. And together they walked into the chamber.

It was an evil sight. A roughly welded grey oval, something like a diver's bell, with four windows for spectators. In the centre stood the metal chair sprouting with heavy leather straps used to secure the arms, chest and legs of the prisoner. At the top was a head restraint and underneath the container for the cyanide and acid which, when combined, would fill the chamber with poisonous fumes. About a dozen grey-faced guards stood around in the small room surrounding the gas chamber. Soon the witnesses would gather there to watch Edward die.

There were only seconds left. The two men stood together for the last time. Clive put his arms around Edward and they hugged each other. As they stood so, Edward whispered in Clive's ear. At first he did not hear. 'Tell me again,' he said. Then he caught it. 'Do you know something that I don't know?' Edward whispered, and looked at Clive with hope still in his eyes. At first Clive did not even understand what he meant. Later he wished he had never understood. Edward, it seemed, still believed that Clive might be able to put a stop to all this. Was it this vain hope that had kept him so calm? Clive did not know and knew not what to say. There was no hope, there would be no more telephone calls, there was nothing now to stop this final act.

Clive mumbled something about Edward knowing about so much more than he would ever know. He could not bring himself even now to crush that still flickering hope. If it helped Edward to die with peace and dignity, surely it was the right thing to do. Then the two men clasped each other in their arms again and said goodbye. As the guards strapped Edward in the chair, Clive looked back on him. He smiled and signed thumbs up. Edward smiled back.

Then Clive was out, outside in the humid summer air. A guard motioned for him to enter the observation room where others were gathering to watch a man die. But he could not bring himself to take those steps. Not yet. He breathed in the air and felt the life in his body. Sandy, who had been waiting outside, came towards him. As he put his arms around her, she burst into tears, letting out the emotions of the past hours she had so bravely withheld. 'I can't go in,' she sobbed. 'Of course, you mustn't,' Clive comforted her. 'There is no need. You have done everything you can for Edward.'

If only someone would say those words to him. But there was no-one left except him. The buck stops here, he thought wryly. He would rather be anywhere in the whole world than in that observation room. But as Edward's lawyer, he should be there. As Edward's friend, he must be there.

He retraced his steps and entered the room. It seemed crowded. There were several people from the press and television who had been invited to witness the event, along with guards and others Clive did not know. He recognised one man as an attorney for the prison whom he had met at a party a year before. But no-one looked in Clive's direction, no-one caught his eye. They turned away from him – ashamed he hoped, but he could not be sure.

Clive was torn between a terrible desire not to look at Edward, now strapped into the chair in the chamber, not to rob him of his dignity at this moment that lacked all dignity, and a desperate belief that his gaze might bring him reassurance, he knew not how. It was Edward's voice that made him look. 'I guess they won't call,' he said. 'I guess they won't call.' There was no need to say more. The others might not know the meaning of the words, but Clive did. Only now had Edward finally given up his hope of the miracle, the phone call from some unknown power releasing him from this nightmare. So Clive looked at his friend but he could not help him. Edward was strapped into the chair so he could not see those who had chosen to watch him die.

Clive never looked again. Even though the minutes dragged by and nothing happened, he kept his eyes averted. Now, after hours of not wanting to see time go by, he wanted every second to go faster. But eight long minutes passed and nothing happened. Then the telephone beside Clive rang and the guard said it was the signal to begin. It was the final tragic irony. Had Edward too heard the harsh ringing of the bell? Had he for a fleeting second thought this was indeed the call that was never to come? In Clive's mind there was no doubt.

It took seventeen minutes for Edward to die. Seventeen minutes before Clive heard the words: 'The prisoner is officially dead.' The words that signalled it was over, over at last. Edward was dead. He who had not known freedom since he was eighteen years old, was free at last.

*   *   *

But for Clive it was not over. It was just a beginning. It was the start and not the end of his involvement with the life of the man who was now dead. Clive did not know it when, barely an hour after Edward's death, his emotions torn between sorrow and anger, he vented some of his feelings on the assembled American media come to hear of the last moments in the life of Edward Earl Johnson; nor did he know it as he drove away from the prison in the early hours of the morning, stopping the car every now and then as his tears overwhelmed him.

But in the days that followed, at home with his wife in Atlanta, as time eased the trauma and dulled the pain, his anger grew at the injustice that had been done. He could not help Edward now, that he knew. But he could not let the case rest. What if he could prove Edward's innocence to the rest of the world? What if he could force the American nation to look at what it had done? What if, by showing them they had killed an innocent man, he could make them question their belief in the death penalty? If he could do that he would not simply have righted the injustice that had been done to Edward, he might also sway public opinion in the USA away from its overwhelming support for capital punishment. And that was Clive's ultimate goal. He had dedicated his life not simply to fighting on behalf of individual prisoners on Death Row, but to the ultimate abolition of the death penalty in the USA.

It is Clive's passionate conviction that state execution is a barbarous act not worthy of a so-called civilised nation. Its use in the USA puts the country in the same category as some of the nations it criticises most bitterly, the USSR and Iran among them. America is the only industrialised, Western country to continue to make use of capital punishment. And in recent years there has been a dramatic increase in the numbers who have died in the execution chambers of the USA. Some of those under sentence of death are juveniles; others are mentally retarded. Critics of the US legal system believe that the use of the death penalty is exercised in an arbitrary manner, factors such as geographical location, politics, social status and race determining whether a convicted murderer should live or die. In Clive's mind, as he reflected on Edward's death in a calmer and more rational manner, the thought took root that proving Edward innocent might also go some way towards proving the iniquity of the death penalty as practised in the United States. If he could do that, Edward's death would not have been in vain. Edward's death could bring hope for other condemned men.

For Clive had no doubts about Edward's innocence. He was sure the young black man had been the victim of racial prejudice and a flawed judicial system. But to prove it he needed evidence, hard evidence that would convince a court if necessary, evidence that no-one had bothered to unearth during the original murder investigation, or had pushed to one side. It would not be easy to find. The killing had happened eight years before, back in 1979. Would the witnesses still be able to remember? Would they want to remember? Would they still be alive? He would have to find out. He would have to go to the small community of Walnut Grove in Leake County, Mississippi, and ask some questions.

It would take time and he had so little to spare. There were many other prisoners depending on him for their lives, waiting in their cells while Clive and a handful of colleagues fought their cases through the courts. There was Edward's namesake, Sam Johnson who also claimed to be innocent of murder and whose appeals were reaching a critical stage. He and Edward had become close friends in Parchman Penitentiary. Sam had suffered like Clive, perhaps more so, the night Edward died. Sam needed

Clive. So too did Leo Edwards, a black man who had been convicted of murder by an all-white jury in Mississippi, and who had been struggling for years to prove that he had been the victim of racial injustice. Leo, too, was a prisoner in Parchman Penitentiary. He had little hope of evading the gas chamber. His life also depended on Clive and lawyers like him. Sam and Leo were alive – still. Edward was dead.

Clive could not turn his back on men like Sam and Leo. For three years he had devoted his life to working for prisoners on Death Row. He knew only too well of the plight facing the hundreds of men and women incarcerated in their prison cells throughout the United States of America and especially in the Southern states, the stronghold of capital punishment. Some of them, too, were no doubt innocent of the crimes for which they had been convicted. Many were not. All, however, were entitled to proper legal counsel and representation.

But it is a right that is all too often vouchsafed in theory and not in practice. These prisoners depended then, and still do, on lawyers like Clive to guide them through the legal maze which is the American judicial system, for most of them are poor and unable to afford the fees normally demanded by American attorneys. Federal and state governments provide little or no financial assistance for prisoners on Death Row, thus effectively depriving them of their constitutional rights. For most prisoners under sentence of death the only hope lies with the pitifully small band of lawyers who are prepared to forego financial reward for the sake of an ideal – that of justice.

Many of these prisoners are doubly disadvantaged. Not only are most of them poor, but many of them are also black, and race can have a direct bearing on the outcome of a trial. In the American Deep South even some judges will admit there is one justice for whites and another for blacks. Memories are still strong of a time, not so many years ago, when blacks were frequently executed without trial. Those days are gone, but the colour of a man's skin still plays a large part in determining his fate. The numbers show that a black man convicted of the murder of a white is many times more likely to end his days in the execution chamber than a white convicted of killing a black.

Clive was well aware of these facts as he agonised over Edward's death. He could not desert men like Sam and Leo, but neither could he leave unchallenged the glaring injustice in which he had been caught up, and which had led to Edward's death. To do so would be to condone the wrongs he believed had been done to the young man whose death he had witnessed; wrongs which, if allowed to continue unchecked, would claim the lives of many other prisoners. Edward had been the victim of a society which would continue to wreak its revenge on the poor and the black of the American Deep South.

Somehow, Clive knew, he would have to stretch his time to serve both the living and the dead. The odds were stacked against him. He did not know if he could find the evidence to prove Edward's innocence. He could hope to save the lives of some of those on Death Row, but it was inevitable that many would die. It was a thankless task. Nevertheless it was a burden he was willing to shoulder.

Two
Clive

For a lawyer to take it upon himself to turn detective for a lost cause is an uncommon turn of events. When lawyers lose a case, as they inevitably must, they turn their attentions to the next, to those that have yet to be decided, to the endless queue of people who need their services. There are few who are prepared to commit their time and efforts in attempting to prove the innocence of a client after the final verdict has been reached, even if they are convinced there has been a gross miscarriage of justice. It takes a man or woman of exceptional dedication and courage to take on such a task.

Clive Stafford Smith is such a man. His determination to continue the fight to clear Edward's name stemmed not only from his love for the black man, but also from his deeply held opposition to the death penalty and his equally deep commitment to his fellow human beings. Clive Stafford Smith's dedication to the abolition of the death penalty approaches fanaticism, and he is proud to admit it. To him the execution of a man or woman by the state is an abhorrence, and he is prepared to go to extraordinary lengths to change the minds of those who do not share his views.

Clive is also a man who is reluctant to admit defeat. Failure is not a part of the vocabulary of this tall, lanky, bespectacled Englishman. Those who stand in his way should not be misled by his deceptively laid-back manner. The jutting chin is a truer pointer to the character within. That he should decide to continue to fight Edward's case, believing as he did that he was innocent, was almost a foregone conclusion given the man he is.

The challenge facing Clive in May 1987 was by far the toughest task he had yet set himself in a life which has taken him from a well-to-do English background to the Death Rows of America's Deep South. But Clive is never one to be daunted, and has proved his ability to reach his goal time and time again during his 30 years – years which have seen a curious

23

ad-mixture of success, achievement and misfortune. He was born with a silver spoon in his mouth but in childhood had to weather the divorce of his parents and the bankruptcy of the family business. He has known both privilege and hardship. By the time of Edward's death in 1987 he had reaped more than his fair share of achievements, due mainly to his own character and abilities rather than his social advantages.

It was in 1978, a year before the killing of Marshal Jake Trest for which Edward Johnson had been sentenced to die, that Clive took his first major step along the road that was to lead to Mississippi. He was eighteen, and still a pupil at Radley College, one of England's most prestigious public schools, when he decided to turn down a place at Cambridge University and go to the United States to study politics and economics at the University of North Carolina. It was a momentous decision, one which changed him much more dramatically than he could ever have envisaged at the time. The man who is now fighting for the lives of America's convicted murderers crossed the Atlantic a relatively conservative product of his upper middle class background. But his early experiences there roused within him thoughts and feelings that were merely waiting to find expression.

Clive went to the United States as a visiting student under the auspices of a fellowship set up by the American industrialist John Morehead, founder of the chemical giant, Union Carbide, a company which achieved notoriety with the Bhopal disaster in India. Known as the Morehead Fellowship, it was open at that time to boys from certain public schools in England, Radley College among them. Three boys a year were chosen from these schools to study at the University of Carolina at Chapel Hill, picked because of its proximity to the centre of the original Union Carbide activities. Clive was one of the successful applicants for this fellowship which allowed him four years at the American university, all expenses paid.

The University of North Carolina, with its main campus at Chapel Hill in the foothills of the Appalachian mountains, is no Ivy League college, but it has a reputation as one of the better public universities in the USA. Its limitations are largely due to its geographical location within one of the Southern states. Traditional Southern conservatism dominates the students' thinking, with new ideas suspect, and not readily accepted. When Clive was a student there, these attitudes were compounded by the fact that by the late 1970s the swing from the radical idealism of the 60s was well under way. US government statistics show that by 1980 the main objective of about two-thirds of all students was to be well-off financially;

the numbers who wanted to develop a meaningful philosophy of life had dropped to half. More than 50 per cent of all students described themselves politically as middle of the road; liberal was a label adopted by a mere 20 per cent. Thus the University of North Carolina was far from being an obvious cradle for the radical liberal philosophy that Clive was to adopt. The university lacked the benefits that can be derived from a cosmopolitan society. Most beliefs went unquestioned because those who were there shared a common outlook, the outside world having little impact. For in common with most American state universities, the vast majority of its students came not only from the USA but from within the state boundaries itself. When Clive arrived at the Chapel Hill campus, of the 20,000 students present a mere fifteen per cent came from 'out of state'. The young Englishman, at six feet four inches tall never one to be lost in a crowd, was destined to be a conspicuous figure around the campus.

'It wasn't so much a culture shock as a lack-of-culture shock,' says Clive, referring to those early months. But despite the drawbacks, Clive now rates his years at Chapel Hill as the most formative of his life. He rapidly became a prominent member of the campus: he joined the staff of the university newspaper and, during his second year, ran for the office of university president.

It was what Clive saw of the United States outside the campus, however, which shaped the direction he was to take in later years. As a Morehead Fellowship student he was obliged to undertake a variety of projects during the summer vacations designed to fit him to be a future leader of men. First-year students were scheduled to take part in an outdoor adventure course before going to university. In the second year, students spent the summer vacation working for a law enforcement agency; in the third they worked for private enterprise; and in the fourth they spent the summer with a government office.

Clive skipped the adventure training course, choosing instead to take a holiday in the south of France. But in his second year he made the most of the opportunities offered to him and went to work with the sheriff's department in Los Angeles. It was an experience which was to stand him in good stead when he later started work as a lawyer. It gave him a privileged insight into the sometimes murky world of American police departments. It also opened his eyes abruptly and brutally to the harsh realities of the outside world. A scene he witnessed and will never forget was the shooting down in cold blood of a drug-crazed youth. 'The guy had a knife and had no idea what he was doing. He was probably dangerous.

But on the other hand there were nine of us and we could have taken care of him without any trouble. But they just blew him away. They could have shot him in the legs. But rather than risk themselves they just killed the guy.'

Other incidents were less traumatic but equally revealing. Clive witnessed first-hand the corruption of American police departments and the extortion rackets in which they were involved. 'They were all crooked and on the take,' he says. 'These guys were the most corrupt group of people I had ever run across. It ranged from petty things like getting free food and coffee everywhere to other stuff which people just hinted at but I didn't see.' Never one to be backward in coming forward, Clive wrote to the sheriff after he returned to university telling him of some of the things he had seen and heard.

Another experience at the police department which was to provide Clive with useful background knowledge in later years was his intro-duction to the polygraph or lie detector test. This device, which is not in common usage in England, is more popular with the authorities in the United States. Information gained from its use is not admissable in evidence in an American court, but at that time it was often brought into play during criminal investigations. For a suspect, the threat of its use could be enough to extract a confession. It appears to have been used in that manner only weeks earlier during a murder investigation in the small town of Walnut Grove, Mississippi, which, eight years later, was to become the focus of Clive's attention, when Edward Earl Johnson was to die in the gas chamber for the killing.

But this twist of fate was unknown to Clive the day he was wired up to the machine in the Los Angeles police department. For Clive it was an opportunity to outwit the machine and prove its unreliability. For others, taking the test in more serious circumstances, it is not such a light-hearted matter. 'It was interesting and convinced me that those things are completely worthless,' is Clive's verdict. 'But for others it can be a dangerous thing. The average Joe on the street thinks that they read your mind. The sensors indicate how nervous you are. Some people get nervous just being hooked up to the machine.' Clive passed the test with flying colours in that the readings gave no indication of whether he was lying or telling the truth. He came up with a formula that was guaranteed to defeat the simple science on which the results were based. 'All I did was sit there thinking erotic thoughts and the little needle went off the scale every time,' he remembers. 'It would never know if you were lying because you were asked a series of questions and if you thought the same thing every time you could say yes or no at random and it just wouldn't be able to tell what you were doing.'

Clive made no friends during his summer with the Los Angeles police, but he had grown with the experience. He returned to his studies no longer a wide-eyed innocent abroad. And he also acquired a piece of information, which was to lead him more directly to his ultimate role as a dedicated opponent of the death penalty. He used to have long arguments with one police officer in particular, who Clive remembers as being rabidly in favour of executing everyone Hispanic or black. During the course of one heated discussion the officer told Clive of an anti-death penalty group in Atlanta called Team Defence. 'If you are one of these communists you should go and work for these people,' he told Clive.

So it was that, the following summer, Clive had his first taste of Death Row. He persuaded those in charge of the Morehead Fellowship programme that the experience of working for Team Defence would be as valid and as valuable as spending the summer with a commercial private enterprise company. It was not what the fellowship had intended but it was certainly enterprising. Team Defence were glad to have him. The organisation needed what help it could get: it consisted only of two lawyers and a secretary working out of a small office in Atlanta, Georgia. They had little money and far from enough time to cope with the huge work-load generated by the increasing numbers of people being sentenced to death in the state. Without any legal background, Clive had to confine himself to a role as a para-legal, visiting the men on Georgia's Death Row, acquiring background information about them and, more importantly, providing them with human contact and friendship. One of the other people who was working for Team Defence at the same time in a similar manner was Andrea Young, daughter of Andrew Young, the black mayor of Atlanta and former American ambassador to the United Nations.

Clive based himself in the small town of Jackson, Georgia, close to the prison and visited Death Row every day. He formed a particularly close relationship with a prisoner by the name of Jack Potts, so much so that the following summer he wrote a book about his life, in which he attempted to tell Jack's story through his own words and those of his family and friends. 'Jack,' says Clive 'is a classic fundamental sociopath. I was trying to put this across in the book.' He recognises now that it was an over-ambitious project, but he was fascinated by Jack's character. 'He has no conscience,' says Clive. 'He lies through his teeth. There is something about him that is just out of tune with everybody else. And yet he is a charming fellow.' So charming in fact that Jack later convinced a woman guard that he should not be killed and persuaded her to bring a gun into the prison so he could escape. Jack did make it out of the prison but his freedom was short-lived: he is still a prisoner on Death Row. But now the student who visited him nine years ago is his laywer. Jack Potts is another for whose life Clive is now battling in the American courts. His appeals are still waiting to be heard.

There were many others who Clive also visited regularly. Some of the prisoners confided in him totally, even going so far as to tell him about their escape plans. 'I never believed them because they were pretty stupid plans,' Clive recalls. 'But then suddenly these four guys escaped doing exactly what they had told me they would do. They had said they would dye their prison uniforms the colour of the guards' uniforms and just walk out. I had laughed and said come on, give me a break. But that is what they did. They just walked out.' The four were recaptured close by shortly afterwards, having found freedom too much for them. 'They got drunk and got caught,' says Clive. He would have advised them to head for Canada, a country which refuses to extradite anybody facing the death penalty. Such was Clive's conviction even then that state execution is an evil and barbarous act that he had few qualms about the possibility of four convicted murderers roaming the country on the run.

Many miles away another young man had also received his introduction to Death Row that summer. Edward Johnson had been convicted of the Walnut Grove murder and taken to the Mississippi State Penitentiary at Parchman from which he was never to be freed.

Following his summer at Death Row, Clive returned to the Chapel Hill campus. But not for long. He was well on target to complete his degree course within the three years he had set himself. After six months he left to return to Jackson and write his book, leaving himself only one course to complete before graduation. He had by now decided where his future lay. He was determined to do what he could to help the hundreds of prisoners on Death Row and, in the long run, help to bring about the abolition of the death penalty in the United States. The most effective way he could see of achieving these aims was to qualify as an American attorney. He was well aware of the poverty of most prisoners on Death Row and the desperate shortage of lawyers willing to take on death penalty cases. They do not bring financial reward and most lawyers are, not unnaturally, unwilling to work without payment. As a lawyer working for those on Death Row who are unable to pay, Clive would be actually saving people's lives. He could not hope to win all his cases, but he could win a reprieve for many and in the course of so doing reveal the death penalty for the iniquity he saw it to be.

So Clive applied for and was offered a place at Columbia University

Law School in New York, one of the country's top Ivy League colleges. As at Chapel Hill, Clive spent much of his time at Columbia in outside activities. His capacity for work seemed limitless. He spent enough time at university to gain himself a law degree, and also became involved in student journalism, as editor of the Columbia newspaper. But his main interests were centred around two organisations in the city. One, the National Association for the Advancement of Coloured People, is a nationwide group founded to promote the interests of black people. The other was the Lawyers' Committee for International Human Rights which represents people seeking refugee status in the United States.

It was while working for this latter organisation that Clive, still a student, wrote his first legal brief. It was an impressive debut. The case was heard in the top court of the land, the United States Supreme Court. But the fairy tale beginning did not have a happy ending, as the case was lost. It was a sad outcome for the client, an East European seeking political asylum, but it was also probably a useful lesson for the fledgling lawyer. Judges are more difficult to convince of the rightness of one's case than most of the people on whom Clive had hitherto exercised his undisputed powers of persuasion. He was disillusioned but not downcast. 'These people are meant to be the brightest in the land,' he says, referring to the judges, 'and yet they had no idea of what the issue was about.' For Clive the serious nature of the issues was a good grounding for his eventual work with prisoners on Death Row. 'Refugee law is somewhat similar to the death penalty,' he says, 'because very often that is what it means when they are sent back.'

He gained experience of legal work on death penalty cases while working for the National Association for the Advancement of Coloured People, known generally as the NAACP. This organisation had been founded in 1909 'to achieve, through peaceful and lawful means, equal citizenship rights for all American citizens by eliminating segregation and discrimination in housing, employment, voting, schools, the courts, transportation and recreation'. It had been active in the civil rights years of the 1950s and 60s in helping black people in their fight for equality under the law. It is still a force to be reckoned with, for despite the fact that American blacks achieved considerable legal changes in those years, the desegregation of schools among them, many of these changes have remained merely superficial. Black people still find themselves disadvantaged, and it is often to the NAACP that they turn when in need of help. (In Edward Johnson's case, for example, the local NAACP leader, who had known him since he was a small boy, organised a fund-raising drive to help pay his legal fees and came to his assistance during his trial, swearing an affidavit as to his good character.) Good lawyers are always needed by the NAACP to help provide legal assistance for poor black people who would otherwise go unrepresented. Clive was a very welcome asset to them.

But it was not all hard work for Clive in New York. During his time at Columbia he met a young Italian girl, Cristiana Ferraro. They married in 1985. By that time Clive had started work as a lawyer for the organisation in Atlanta, Georgia, where he is still based. He graduated from Columbia in 1984 and almost immediately joined the Southern Prisoners' Defence Committee, a charitably funded group of lawyers who work solely for condemned prisoners unable to afford legal help. Their mission is two-fold: to represent accused and convicted murderers, and to try and better the conditions of those on Death Row throughout the Southern states. The organisation was founded in 1976 with offices in New Orleans, Louisiana, and Nashville, Tennessee. At that time it consisted only of two lawyers who spent most of their time working to better prison conditions. However, as the numbers of those facing death through execution rose, following a decision by the US Supreme Court to allow individual states to re-enact death penalty legislation that had early in the 1970s been declared unconstitutional, SPDC found itself increasingly in demand by those awaiting death.

In 1981 a young Kentucky lawyer by the name of Steve Bright took over the running of the group and moved the offices to Atlanta in the heart of an area where the judicial and public demand for the imposition of death sentences was particularly great. Steve, who is still in charge, is a highly experienced lawyer. Before moving to SPDC he spent several years with the nation's premier public defender group in Washington DC, and then went on to teach at law school. Like Clive and all the others working for SPDC, he is a dedicated opponent of the death penalty. Under his influence the organisation started to expand so that at one time it employed the services of eight lawyers. The budget, however, did not increase. The group is funded by the Clark Foundation in New York and the Public Welfare Foundation in Washington DC. Money is in short supply. As the numbers working for SPDC went up, salaries went down as the same funds were shared between more people. It was a relief to the hard-pressed group when Clive persuaded Columbia University to pay his first year's salary at SPDC. It also demonstrated the esteem in which Clive is held by those who have been involved with his education throughout the years.

The cramped and run-down offices in downtown Atlanta, which are the headquarters of SPDC, now house four lawyers working on death penalty cases, two working on prison conditions, and three or four administrative staff. Of these Clive is now the second longest serving member after Steve Bright, as the turnover is relatively high. The work is physically and emotionally demanding and takes its toll on those who bear the strain. Steve, who is only 40, has suffered two heart attacks: others have been forced to leave through ill health.

Even Clive is beginning to feel his great reserves of energy under strain. He was deluged with work as soon as he joined the Atlanta team in 1984. It was a case of going in at the deep end from the top diving board while blindfolded. By the fourth month he was handling a death penalty case by himself. 'It is a ridiculous situation. It is absurd to put someone with so little experience in that position. But it is just that there is no alternative because there is no-one else to do it,' he says. 'You learn quickly. You have to.' He admits he made many mistakes along the way, for it was a bad time in some ways for him to join the group. 'There was a real pressure of executions at the time. They executed two of our clients within the first six months I was there.' Since then he has been involved in many cases, probably more than 100, almost half of which are still on-going. Such is the length of the appeal system in the United States that it can take up to twelve years before it is exhausted. He used to work eighteen hours a day before Cristiana came to live in Atlanta, and his hours now are not vastly reduced. He takes few holidays and travels hundreds of thousands of miles every year, often by bus for the sake of cost, criss-crossing the Southern states in the interests of his clients.

These include Judy Houston, the only woman on Death Row in the state of Mississippi. She was convicted in 1985 of strangling her fourteen-year-old daughter in a fit of rage after the young girl had accused her mother of having an affair with a family friend. Clive took over the case 18 months later after the original trial lawyers had withdrawn. The strongest plank in the appeals he has lodged on Judy Houston's behalf is the trial judge's refusal to allow most of her defence witnesses to testify on her behalf at the trial. Of the 46 witnesses, about 40 were barred for technical reasons. If they had been allowed to give evidence, Clive believes they would have provided a truer picture of Judy Houston and of the events leading up to the murder of her daughter. The jury would have heard how, far from being a violent woman herself, Judy Houston was the victim of brutal attacks by her husband. She was a battered wife who had snapped when taunted by her daughter. At the end of 1988 Clive won his appeal to have Judy Houston's conviction and sentence overturned. The Mississippi Supreme Court ordered a retrial, which has yet to be heard. The state is asking for a reimposition of the death penalty. This time, Clive intends that Judy Houston's side of the story should be heard.

Hundreds of miles away, on Death Row in Georgia, is yet another client whose ultimate fate rests in Clive's hands. Nicky Ingram was sentenced to death on his twentieth birthday in 1983 for murdering a man in the course of a robbery. The two men, lawyer and prisoner, have a curious connection, for both were born in the same English hospital in Cambridge. Nicky Ingram, the son of an Englishwoman now divorced from her American husband, is the only man on Death Row with claims to British citizenship. In December, 1988, while Clive was in England visiting his family for Christmas, an American court saw fit to set an execution date for Nicky Ingram, despite the fact that his appeals against sentence were still outstanding. Clive returned to the USA in time to win a stay of execution only hours before the sentence was due to be carried out. It was a situation to which he has become accustomed. Many of his clients face repeated execution dates during the course of Clive's legal manoeuvres through the appeal system. These days he takes it in his stride. But for the individuals concerned it is a harrowing experience.

Clive spends most of his time representing prisoners after they have been convicted. He believes that he can be more effective at the appeal rather than the trial stage, firstly because of the frequent lack of any legal assistance after conviction and secondly because he can handle more appeals than he can trials. The sheer volume of work involved in a trial makes it a time-consuming affair. Occasionally, however, he finds himself drawn into a case from its start. One such is that of a black man called Willie Gamble, who was charged with murder in the course of robbery. Willie Gamble is from a small rural town in the south of Georgia. He is a believer in voodoo, a form of sorcery which has taken a grip of many of his race in the Southern states. Clive has discovered that Willie Gamble believed he was under a voodoo curse at the time he committed the crime. It was a factor given little weight by the all-white jury which tried the case. Clive lost on that occasion but has succeeded in his efforts to have a re-trial ordered on the grounds that Willie Gamble was the victim of racial prejudice because of the composition of the trial jury. Clive's work on this case, as on others, has taken him outside the boundaries normally associated with a lawyer's work. Inevitably many hours are spent in the office compiling legal briefs, but Clive has also devoted many hours to the investigation of the events leading up to the crime and has attended civil rights meetings to rally support among the black community in the area.

Clive's commitment to his clients puts tremendous strains on his personal life. It is not easy to be married to a man with a mission. His wife Cristiana spends many nights alone in their small house in Atlanta, which lies in a black area of the city. It is cheap, shabby and, for Clive and Cristiana, affordable. Cristiana is nervous of being alone in the house despite the fact that since a recent burglary it has been fortified with alarms and locks to make it almost impregnable. That burglary took place while Clive was in Mississippi fighting against the clock to save Edward Johnson's life. In the middle of the night, about a week before Edward died, Clive received a panic-stricken call to say that Cristiana had returned home from a party to find the front door literally smashed in and everything of any value gone. The next morning Clive went to see Edward in his Death Row cell and told him what had happened. 'You should go home,' the prisoner awaiting execution told his attorney. 'That was just typical of the kind of man he was,' says Clive. 'He had only a week to live yet he told me to go home.' So that afternoon Clive set off on the 500-mile journey to Atlanta. He arrived about 4.00 am, spent the day putting a new door on the house and adding some bars to it so it could not be smashed down again, then set off back to Mississippi at 4.00 the following morning.

Cristiana also worries that one day she may be visited at home by some of Clive's clients. 'The question you have to ask yourself, whatever you may think about the death penalty and however much you get along with some of the prisoners, is "Would you want them to come round for dinner one night?".' Clive would make them welcome. Cristiana would not. She has increasingly divorced herself from the world of murder and execution which consumes Clive's time and energies.

*   *   *

It is all a far cry from Clive's childhood. He was born in the university city of Cambridge on July 9th 1959, the third child of Dick and Jean Stafford Smith. It was a memorable birth in more than one respect. Clive was born a Rhesus baby and survived thanks to a life-saving blood transfusion. 'I often think it must have been exceptional blood,' his mother says today.

The Stafford Smiths ran one of the premier stud farms in England. Clive was brought up on a rolling 360-acre estate on the outskirts of the famous Suffolk horseracing town of Newmarket. Cheveley Park Stud is one of the oldest stud farms in the world, with parish records dating back to the year 940. For many years it belonged to the Dukes of Rutland and, at one time in its history, the monarchs of the day brought their mares there. It was in many ways an idyllic setting in which to bring up a family. Clive, his brother Mark and sister Mary, with only three years separating them, were free to roam through the parklands, there were ponies to ride, and later old cars to drive around the estate's private roads.

But not long after Clive was born the cracks started to appear in his seemingly happy family life. Clive's father had inherited the stud from his father, in trust with his sister. Dick was full of grandiose ideas for the stud's development, but they all demanded money. Dick Stafford Smith is a charming, intelligent man who had no difficulty in raising the capital required, but he was not successful in turning these ideas into reality. The debts grew, and so did the friction within the family, with Clive's mother and paternal aunt on one side and his father on the other. They were turbulent years in which the children were very much involved. Clive's father did not believe in shielding his children from his problems, rather the reverse. He actively involved them in the disputes that arose, at one time calling all three home from their boarding schools to win their support for his plans to borrow more money against the opposition of his wife and sister.

Thus, as a child of ten, Clive was being asked to make decisions on complex financial matters involving conflicting family loyalties that most adults would find hard to cope with. The tensions within the family grew and by the time Clive was twelve years old his parents had decided to divorce. Dick Stfford Smith departed from Cheveley Park Stud and his family, leaving his wife and sister to try and salvage the business from financial ruin. But, with debts running into hundreds of thousands of pounds, it proved an impossible task, despite the best efforts of Clive's mother to save the situation. Bankruptcy was inevitable and when Clive was fifteen years old the Official Receiver was called in. Clive and his family moved into a small house in Cambridge which his mother had managed to secure from the creditors.

These were unhappy and traumatic years for Clive, coinciding as they did with his own adolescent development, but they played an important part in forming the man he is today. He can trace many of his beliefs from these childhood experiences and especially from the influence of his father whom Clive looks upon with affection despite his shortcomings, and acknowledges as the person who has most influenced his own life.

The family financial problems help to explain why money takes such a low priority in Clive's own life today. As an American attorney he could now be a relatively wealthy man instead of existing as he does on an average secretary's wage. But he learned at an early age to associate being well off with a fairly miserable existence. He discovered a happier life after the bankruptcy and his parents' divorce, when money was in short supply. Consequently, he says, he now has little respect for money. But Clive is also wise enough to acknowledge that it is easier for one who has known wealth to reject it than for those who have always been poor.

His moral outlook, too, Clive traces back to his father. Dick Stafford Smith treated his children as adults from an early age, not only by involving them in family disputes, but more positively by encouraging them to think about and discuss philosophical issues. He impressed upon them the fact that they were privileged children and had a duty to help society. It was his habit to write moral tracts on his own beliefs for his children to read. Looking back on it now, Clive remembers his father as a man with an original mind, whose failing was that he never managed to live up to his own standards.

The Stafford Smith children were protected from some of the family conflict because of their absence from home at their respective schools. Clive followed his brother Mark from his prep school to Radley College where, like his brother, he won a scholarship. It is a reflection on the brothers' abilities that, when the family ran into difficulties, the school waived the fees in order to enable the children to remain. The headmaster of Radley College, known as the warden, is and was then the distinguished educationalist, Dennis Silk. He remembers Clive as the outstanding boy of his generation at the school. 'Academically he was very strong, and was one of the few boys who could have walked into Oxford or Cambridge,' says Dennis Silk today. But he was more than just a clever pupil. He was also, at that stage of his life, extremely determined and, according to Dennis Silk, had an unusually enlightened view of events and society. He was a constant supporter of the underdog. Such were Clive's all-round abilities that in the fifth form he was voted the boy most likely to succeed and subsequently in the sixth form chosen to be senior prefect, the school's equivalent of head boy.

When Clive left Radley, he left his past behind him, and he has few, if any, close friends from those days. There was little to bind him to his classmates, most of whom moved on to jobs in the City and other Establishment positions. The difficulty for Clive during his last two years at school had been finding his own direction without compass or signposts. Thanks to his decision to continue his studies in the USA, instead of Cambridge, he was eventually to find his mission in life, not in the boardrooms of Britain but in the prisons of an alien and foreign land – the American Deep South.

Three
Troubled Times

The Southern states of American are, in many ways, in name only a part of the union that is the USA. The Confederate flag still flies proudly in many areas of the Deep South. It is a region that has continued to hang on to its own identity despite the fact that more than a century has passed since the Confederate army was defeated in the American Civil War, and the people of the South were dragged back into a reluctant partnership with their Yankee cousins. The Deep South still clings tenaciously to its self-perceived independence. Many Southerners consider the union has brought them few benefits, and states such as Mississippi and Alabama rank among the poorest in the nation. The descendants of the original settlers look back fondly on the days of the great plantations when, for some whites at least, life was good. They regret the end of the prosperity that was forged on the backs of the black slaves. They regret also the rulings of the Federal government that have decreed they should now live as equals with their fellow black citizens. Poverty and inbred racial prejudice have done little to bring harmony to this part of America that is a backwater of the nation's life.

It was into this world, on June 22nd 1960, that a baby was born whose life would illustrate the social and economic divisions that are still prevalent in the American Deep South today. On that day, shortly before Clive celebrated his first birthday in England, a young woman gave birth to a baby many thousands of miles away. Few young lives could have contrasted more starkly with Clive's comfortable existence than that of this little boy. He was born in extreme poverty in Jackson, the state capital of Mississippi, into a society that would label him inferior from the minute he drew his first breath. This baby was black. He was named Edward Earl Johnson.

There was little that was to be easy in the short life of Edward Johnson, and his birth was no exception. The baby was born six weeks prematurely, weighing a mere three pounds, five ounces. He could have died then, but he didn't. For four weeks he survived in a hospital incubator and eventually was pronounced strong enough to be allowed home with his 20-year-old mother, Bettye Lou. Home was a cramped apartment in a run-down black section of the Mississippi state capital. Edward's father, known as JB, was an unskilled laundry worker. His mother did domestic work as well as holding down a job at a poultry company in order to make ends meet. The couple had always been poor but now they were at their wits' end worrying how to pay the medical bills that Edward's birth had incurred. Bettye Lou had no alternative but to carry on working after the baby returned home, leaving him in the care of a child minder.

This arrangement, however, was short-lived. The marriage was far from happy. JB had started drinking heavily shortly after the wedding, frequently staying away from home for days at a time. When he returned it was often only to ask for more money, a demand that led to violent arguments. Edward's birth was most probably precipitated by one such row, the confrontation ending when Bettye Lou, seven months pregnant, was kicked in the stomach.

Edward was about six weeks old when Bettye Lou's parents came to visit the baby from their home in the rural community of Walnut Grove, about 50 miles away from Jackson. Bettye Lou was at work when they arrived and Edward was at home with the child minder. They found the sickly infant lying in soiled clothes crying from hunger. Phinas and Jessie Mae Lewis were distressed by what they saw. They were simple country people who, despite extreme poverty, had struggled to rear their own five children as best they could. They told their daughter that she could not care for the baby properly while working full-time and suggested that he should return home with them. As Jessie Mae was to tell Clive many years later following her grandson's death: 'It was too hard for her to care for him right, what with her working all the time and leaving him with a babysitter. She wasn't taking care of him properly. She wasn't feeding him right or nothing.'

Bettye Lou accepted that her parents were right. For about a year she attempted to keep in contact with her son, travelling up from Jackson at weekends when she could. But then, by this time parted from her husband, she decided like thousands before her that she must move north if she was ever to have a chance of a decent life. The Deep South in the 1960s could offer black people little but trouble. Bettye Lou took up one of the few options open to black Southern women and moved to New York to work as a live-in domestic help.

Little Edward settled in well with his grandparents in his new home. The family lived in a small wooden house typical of the area about five miles from Walnut Grove. The town, if such it can be called, lies deep within the Mississippi heartland in Leake County, one of the most deprived and backward areas in a state which is still today the poorest in the nation. Its residents earn a meagre living from the land, farming cotton and a mixture of other crops. The flat, wooded landscape is intersected by numerous creeks, rivers and swamps. It is a depressed and depressing area. The few score wooden homes which make up Walnut Grove itself have today a relatively neat and tidy air about them, but the countryside around is dotted with dilapidated shacks, held together with pieces of corrugated iron and other assorted oddments, that would fit unnoticed into a Third World shanty town. It is far from obvious to the passing traveller that this is a part of the richest nation on earth. A dirt road is all that leads to the huddle of three houses deep among the scrub and woods where Jessie Mae still lives. The community has been blessed with the name of Standing Pine, but a stranger unaware of its existence would be unlikely to find it.

Edward quickly became very attached to his grandmother, whom he always called Momma. Jessie Mae was a woman of strong character who set high standards. She had brought up her own children to be well-behaved and hard-working, as she was herself, and she applied the same rules to Edward. The elderly couple worked as sharecroppers, eking out a living by tenant farming and paying the owner rent in the form of a share of the crop. The system was also known as 'working on halves' as the owner of the land received 50 per cent of the money earned from the harvest. The sharecropper meanwhile had to pay for next year's seed and all other expenses out of his half. Jessie Mae also took in laundry and cleaned houses to make ends meet. It was a hard life. The five Lewis children would have to work on the farm as well and only attended school spasmodically. In the rural areas of Mississippi it was the way most children lived.

The Lewis' eldest son Nathaniel was still living at home when Edward arrived. He joined the exodus north shortly afterwards in an attempt to better himself, and now lives in Chicago where he owns his own truck business. Whereas he was lucky to get a few weeks of schooling a year, his children have college educations. He remembers his childhood as a constant struggle. 'We never had any money and I would only get to go to school after November or early December when the harvest was in. Then I would have to quit again in March when the winter was over and it was time to get back out to the fields. My father was still hard at work up until the time he died in 1982.'

Life was not much different for Edward 20 years on. He was able to attend school more regularly, but he was still required to supplement the family income from a very early age. At a time when Clive's bags were being packed for preparatory school in England, Edward was already working in the fields. 'He was about seven when he started working odd jobs,' Jessie Mae told Clive during one of his frequent visits to her Walnut Grove home in the course of his investigations on Edward's behalf. 'He started working with the chickens. He thought of himself as the "boss of the chickens". I would let him work in the morning before school. After school he would be glad to go back to work but I made him do his homework. When he got a little older I would let him do some work after school. He would work in the summertime too. He would get paid about a dollar a day. That wasn't bad considering no-one, even grown-ups, was getting much at that time.'

One local farmer remembers Edward doing odd jobs for him from about the age of nine. 'He would help me haul hay, fix fences, build barns and do other things that a farm's upkeep would call for,' he said. 'He was a good worker. He never gave me a moment of trouble. He never sassed. He was always a respectful person.' These things count for much in the South.

The next few years passed without any further dramatic upheavals for Edward. He had not been a healthy baby − 'sick and weesey' was Jessie Mae's description − and the family called him Squeakie because he was so small. He grew stronger as he grew older but he was never to lose the nickname. The major event in his early years was a trip to New York when he was four to see his mother. She wanted him to stay, but he was keen to return home with the woman he thought of as his mother. 'I remember when I was packing my things to return to Mississippi, I had my stuff laid out on the bed,' Jessie Mae told Clive. 'The next thing I knew Edward Earl was laying his things out on the bed with mine. I asked what he was doing and he said that he was packing to go home with me. When his mother asked if he wasn't going to stay with her, he said that he had to go home to take care of Momma.'

So Edward returned to Walnut Grove. In retrospect it would have been better if he had remained in New York. He might still be alive today.

*   *   *

The boy's own childhood may have been uneventful but the opposite was the case in Mississippi at the time. Edward was to grow up in an area which witnessed turbulence, violence and prejudice such as had not been seen since the American Civil War 100 years before. The 1960s were years which tore the fragile union of the USA apart, pitting white against black, Southerner against Yankee in a manner that was to leave deep scars on those who lived through that troubled time, scars that are still evident today. They were the years of the great civil rights movement during which black people fought a bitter battle to abolish segregation and overturn the legal inequities with which they had lived since their freedom from slavery. Southern whites ferociously opposed the threat they saw to their way of life. Many had grandparents who could remember the war that was fought against the Yankees. One of the causes they fought for then was their right to keep their blacks in slavery, contrary to the demands of the North. Their descendants, it seemed at times, were willing to fight that war again.

The blacks had won their first major victory in the civil rights fight in 1954 when the United States Supreme Court ruled that segregated schools contravened the US constitution. The judges concluded in the case of Brown versus the Board of Education of Tepeka that in the field of public education the doctrine of separate but equal had no place. 'Separate educational facilities are inherently unequal,' they said. Civil rights leaders were delighted by the result but soon realised it had little effect in practice. Few Southern states made any attempt to integrate their schools: they were not going to be told what to do by some interfering judges; they would run their affairs how they wanted to. The issue in the end had to be fought in the school grounds and buildings rather than the court rooms. An historic and violent confrontation took place in Little Rock, Arkansas, in 1957 when the National Guard was brought in to protect nine black schoolchildren from white protestors after they announced their intention to enrol at the town's Central High School.

The battle ground was also widened to other areas of everyday life where blacks were treated as second-class citizens. Segregated buses were the norm in the Southern states. The whites sat at the front, the blacks at the back. When the white section filled up blacks were ordered to move further back and give up their seats to the whites. In an attempt to end this inequity, the blacks in Montgomery, Alabama, organised a boycott of buses that was to last for thirteen months and ended when the US Supreme Court ruled that segregated buses were unlawful. It was again a violent struggle. Houses were bombed, buses were fired on, blacks were imprisoned. One of the leaders of that protest was a young minister called Martin Luther King Jr, who was to become the leader of the black movement and lose his own life in the process, felled by an assassin's bullet.

In Mississippi white reaction to the black demands was especially virulent. The state was probably the most white supremacist and segregated in the country. The 1954 decision on segregated schools resulted in beatings, burnings and lynchings. White supremacists' opposition to the civil rights movement and the rulings of the country's top court saw the resurgence of a secret society which had been born at the end of the Civil War to promote white Anglo-Saxon supremacy. It was called the Ku Klux Klan. Its members wear white robes and hoods to disguise their identity, and believe in using violence to achieve their aims.

National attention was focussed on the state in 1955 when a fourteen-year-old black boy was murdered after being cheeky to a white shop assistant. Emmett Till, who came from Chicago, had been visiting relatives and was unused to Southern white attitudes to black people. He paid for his ignorance with his life. All too frequently when blacks were murdered the crimes never came to court but, because of the national publicity, two white men were charged with his murder. The case was heard in the small community of Sumner, only a few miles from the present site of the Mississippi State Penitentiary at Parchman, where Edward Johnson was to meet his death 32 years later. The all-white jury brought in a not guilty verdict, which caused uproar among blacks and in the North, but failed to right what had appeared to be a glaring injustice.

For many Mississippi blacks at that time life seemed hopeless. The population of the state was 45 per cent black but the system was weighted against them and only 5 per cent were registered to vote. They had no power, as they were barred from the ballot box. During the last five years of the 1950s, 315,000 Mississippi blacks migrated north, many of Edward Johnson's relatives among them. They chose to leave their homes where they had little chance of an education or a job, to seek a future in the more liberal, less segregated North.

Edward's father, JB Johnson, was one of those who stayed. It is little wonder that he found solace in the bottle. 'There was very little that I could have done in Walnut Grove at that time,' he says looking back on those years. 'It was a very closed community to a black man who wanted to make something of himself. The schools were not desegregated for years after I left. The only jobs you could hope to get would be on a farm or odd jobs. People would pay you a little and give you some food out under a tree, but in those days a black man could not go inside to eat the food. One night I had gone with a friend to a nearby town and we were about to drive back to Walnut Grove when the police pulled us over saying my friend was speeding, which was not true. They took him off to jail and he did not get out until the next day. They told me to walk home – that was about twelve miles. That was the way it was in the county.'

JB Johnson did not know it then, but he was lucky to be able to walk home that night. The fate awaiting three others pulled over for speeding in the same area a few years later was a gruesome and brutal death. By the time the now notorious murder of three civil rights workers occurred, on Edward's fourth birthday, the state of Mississippi had already achieved worldwide notoriety for its violent opposition to black civil rights and its flagrant flouting of the laws of the country. A *cause célèbre* that hit the international headlines was that of a young black man called James Meredith. In 1962 he was a student at the all-black Jackson State University, but he wished to attend the all-white University of Mississippi where he would receive a vastly superior education. Ole Miss, as the university is known, was a hallowed temple of Mississippi history and tradition. It stood for everything valued by Southerners still hankering after pre-Civil War days when plantation owners ruled the land in elegant opulence, blacks knew their place, and Northerners had no say in the running of the state. The university mascot was 'Colonel Reb', a symbolic Confederate Army general. Ole Miss refused to admit James Meredith despite being ordered to do so by a federal court.

The university was backed by the Governor of Mississippi, Ross Barnett, who went on television to oppose the court ruling. This, he said, is the 'moment of our greatest crisis since the war between the states. We must either submit to the unlawful dictate of the federal government or stand up like men and tell them never.' The then President, John F Kennedy, became personally involved in the dispute and it was eventually agreed that Meredith would be smuggled into the university and his admittance would be announced as a *fait accompli*. Hundreds of police were moved on to the campus to control the anticipated storm of protest that such a move would inevitably bring. But when the rioting started the Mississippi highway patrolmen, who made up the bulk of the campus force, left the scene and failed to return despite demands from the White House that Governor Barnett should order them to do so. Instead Barnett again went on television where he spoke in terms used by nations at war. 'You are trampling on the sovereignty of this great state,' he declared, referring to the US Government. 'I call on Mississippi to keep faith and courage. We will never surrender.' Pitched battles were by now raging at Ole Miss. Kennedy had no alternative but to order in the troops, an action he had been loath to take for fear of playing into the Governor's hands. By the time order was restored, scores of people had been injured, hundreds arrested and at least two were dead.

James Meredith won his right to an education and established an important principle in the fight against segregation, but it was a victory where the winner paid dearly. The conflict left a deep and abiding resentment among Mississippi whites which was felt by the whole of the black community. The hatred surfaced dramatically in June, 1966, when James Meredith returned to the state for only the second time since his graduation. He was shot a few miles inside the Mississippi state line after being passed by a car carrying whites waving the Confederate flag. Meredith survived to tell the tale.

One of the men who supported Meredith in his struggle was Medgar Evers, the local leader of the NAACP, the group for which Clive was later to work as a student. He lived in Jackson and had long been active in the civil rights movement. In 1963, a year after the Ole Miss riots, Medgar, a local hero in the eyes of many black people, was shot dead as he was getting out of a car outside his house. Rioting followed the news of his death, with demonstrators clashing with police after the funeral. Medgar was buried at Arlington National Cemetery in Washington DC and his widow received the personal condolences of President Kennedy, who himself had only a few months to live. A white man from a small town north of Jackson was charged with his murder but was acquitted.

Despite Medgar's death, the NAACP continued and stepped up its campaign to have black people registered as voters. At that time Mississippi law stated that, in order to qualify to vote, a person must be able to read and interpret the state constitution. This meant in practice that few black people were deemed eligible to use their right to vote. They could be questioned on their knowledge of the constitution and it was a simple matter to rule that they did not have sufficient understanding of this complicated legal document.

One black lawyer active in the campaign in Mississippi at the time was R Jess Brown, who was later to represent Edward Johnson at his trial for the Walnut Grove murder. Today he is an old man living in a shabby black suburb of Jackson. But, despite age and ill health, he still retains some of the fire he once had in his heart. A small, slight man, with a shock of white hair, European features and a very pale skin, he will harangue an unsuspecting visitor with all the vehemence he can muster. It is a one-sided debate as Jess Brown has become very deaf in his old age, a fact which was to hamper him enormously during Edward's trial.

But, in 1964 when Jess was in his early fifties and unimpeded by physical disability, he was a leading member of the civil rights movement in Mississippi. Shortly after James Meredith won his personal victory against racism to become a student at Ole Miss, Jess had taken up the case of a second black student, Cleve McDowell, who wished to study at the Ole Miss Law School. Meredith's victory had by no means opened the door to black students. Jess had to fight Cleve's case every inch of the way, not only to have the young man accepted at the university, but also to protect him from intimidation once he was there. The threats against Cleve were not purely physical. At one point when driving through one of the state's rural counties, Cleve was pulled over for speeding by a white policeman. The case went to court with Jess Brown defending. The officer claimed there had been a high-speed chase before the young black was stopped. But after relentless cross-examination, Jess Brown was able to show that if what the policeman said was true, the chase had taken place over poor country roads at an average speed of just over 200 mph. Cleve is now regional field director for the NAACP in Mississippi and is involved in working on a death penalty case with Clive Stafford Smith. 'The paths of the liberal clique cross rather frequently in a state where there are so few of them,' says Clive.

At around the same time he was fighting for Cleve McDowell, Jess Brown was also taking a leading role in the registration campaign in Mississippi. 'Trying to register as a voter was a ridiculous situation,' says Jess, looking back on those turbulent times. 'It was a case of the blind leading the blind as the court clerk responsible for making the decision was probably only educated to about fourth grade himself.'

The organisers of the campaign decided to run a massive voter registration drive in 1964 bringing in hundreds of young people from the Northern states to help make black people aware of their rights, encourage them to register and give them moral support. The campaign was to be known as Freedom Summer. Jess Brown warned the out-of-state youngsters, most of them white students, of the dangers they faced in their work. 'If you're riding down somewhere and a cop stops you and starts to put you under arrest, even though you haven't committed any crime, go to jail. Mississippi is not the place to start conducting constitutional law classes for the policemen.'

The first wave of volunteers was sent out into the Mississippi countryside on June 21st. The next day three of them were reported missing. They were Andrew Goodman from New York City, Michael Schwerner from Brooklyn and black Mississippian called James Chaney.

They left from the town of Meridian, one of the state's larger communities, which was the home of James Chaney. The morning they departed the trio attended a service at St Paul's Episcopalian Church. The minister at that church today is a priest called Henry Hudson, who for several years was in charge of the parish of Sumner near the Mississippi State Penitentiary and was the first minister to include the prisoners on Death Row among his flock. As a regular visitor of the condemned men, he knew Edward Johnson well. As with Jess Brown, once again the threads of the civil rights movement in the 1960s have woven a connecting pattern around the fate of the young black man which weighs so heavily on the heart and mind of Clive Stafford Smith.

No-one has ever discovered exactly what happened to the three civil rights workers after they left the Meridian church. All that is absolutely certain is that their bodies were found underneath an earthen dam on August 4th. All had been shot with .38 calibre bullets, and the black man had also been savagely beaten. It is believed that after they left Meridian their station wagon was stopped for speeding by a deputy sheriff near the small town of Philadelphia, Mississippi, about 20 miles from Walnut Grove, and they were taken to the town jail. It is also thought that they were released later that night. But for weeks it appeared that thereafter they had simply vanished into thin air.

Workers at Freedom Summer headquarters, though, knew they were in trouble when they failed to ring in that night at the appointed time as they had been trained to do. The FBI and the local police were alerted, and once again national interest focussed on the Deep South state. The investigation was handed over to the FBI, and 200 sailors were drafted in to search the endless swamps and creeks of Mississippi for the three young men. The wife of Michael Schwerner commented at the time: 'It is tragic that white Northerners have to be caught up into the machinery of injustice and indifference in the South before the American people register concern. I personally suspect that if Mr Chaney, who is a native Mississippian, had been alone at the time of the disappearance, that this case, like so many others would have gone completely unnoticed.'

Despite the intensive search and the interrogation of local police and whites the bodies were only discovered after a tip-off. And it was only in December that any arrests were made. Among the 21 white Mississippians taken into custody was the deputy sheriff who had stopped the dead men's car for speeding. The number also included several local whites thought to have close connections with the Ku Klux Klan. Murder charges were brought against some of the defendants, but they were later dropped although six of the men were later given prison sentences for violating federal civil rights laws.

Among the many tragedies and horrific crimes that occurred during the years of the civil rights campaign, this was undoubtedly one of the worst. In 1989 a film was released in Britain and the United States, which relives the violence and fear among the local communities at that time. Called *Mississippi Burning*, it portrays the murder of the young men in graphic detail as well as the ensuing intimidation of blacks in the area who might have been able to reveal vital knowledge to the FBI. It also lays the killing squarely at the door of the deputy sheriff and his cronies. But the truth of what happened has been buried as deeply as were the bodies under the dam on a Mississippi farm.

Freedom Summer volunteers continued their campaign despite the tragic and barbarous death of their colleagues. That year the Mississippi Freedom Democratic Party was founded to challenge the established Democratic Party which in practice refused membership to blacks. By the August of 1964, 80,000 blacks had joined the MFDP. The campaign had succeeded beyond all expectations in arousing the political consciousness of black people in the state. Freedom Summer workers even managed to convince a few white people to join the party, although they were regarded with extreme resentment by the bulk of the white population. Delegates of the newly formed party attended the Democratic National Convention in Atlantic City where Lyndon Johnson was nominated as the presidential candidate. They challenged the right of the delegates from the official Democratic Party to represent the state and in so doing caused uproar on the floor of the convention hall.

Ten years had now passed since the black civil rights movement had achieved its first major breakthrough. It appeared to have come a long way since then. In 1964 a Civil Rights Act was passed ending discrimination against blacks in employment, restaurants and other public places, and bodies such as trade unions and professional organisations. President Johnson told the nation that the days of denying rights to black people were over. 'Let us close the springs of racial poison,' he said. The following year the Voting Rights Act was signed, aimed at abolishing all restrictions used to deny people the right to vote. These were major measures, but they were to be the pinnacle of achievement.

By the middle of the decade the mood was changing, not only in the United States but throughout the world. The next five years were to see the rise of the anti-Vietnam War movement in the US and allied countries, and the growth of mass protest. The fight against racism in America was not over but it spread its tentacles into the cities of the North, and violence and rioting became the weapon of the first rather than the last resort. The early civil rights workers had been on the receiving end of violence but had rarely resorted to its use themselves. Now there was a swing against the pacifist approach. The catchwords of the day were 'Black Power' as epitomised by the extremist Black Panther group. The struggle also had to share the stage with a host of other causes and the spotlight was to be less frequently directed at the Southern states. It would take events of great magnitude, such as the murder of Nobel Peace Prize winner, Martin Luther King Jr, to bring the world's press flocking once again to the area.

With the advent of the 1970s and the eventual right-wing swing against the protest movements and radicalism in general, the condition of black people in the South was to slide further and further into the recesses of the nation's consciousness. For many Americans it ceased to be a major issue. Had not blacks after all won their fight against segregation and discrimination? Were not the schools legally open to all? Were there not black judges, senators and mayors? Was this not now a country where all were free and had equal rights? Should not the nation's conscience and sense of righteousness be directed against the anti-apartheid laws of South Africa and the persecution of human rights activists in the USSR?

Four
Murder in Walnut Grove

For a young black man such as Edward Johnson, however, the society in which he lived seemed notably lacking in the freedom and equality the civil rights activists had fought so hard to obtain. Within the narrow confines of his rural Mississippi life, desegregation was a meaningless concept for the majority of his white neighbours. He was to experience the full reality of racial prejudice in the Deep South when, at the age of eighteen, he was plucked from his home and family to be tried and convicted of the murder of the Walnut Grove town marshal, Jake Trest.

Attitudes die hard in the American Deep South. Judges and legislators may change the laws but they cannot change the prejudices and opinions of the ordinary man. What is 20 or 30 years of racial desegregation to a Mississippi white who still, when he refers to 'before the war', means before the Civil War of more than 100 years before? Is it not unrealistic to expect that the descendants of the Confederate Army soldiers, who still hold a grudge against the Northern Yankees, should in a few short years come to regard their black neighbours as their equals, blacks who for decades they had treated as inherently inferior and in some cases sub-human?

There are many whites in the North today who would like to think that times have changed. There are many blacks in the South who will tell you it is not the case. There are many Southerners who will go along with the pretence while harbouring the same prejudices that the civil rights movements fought so hard to break down. As one charming Alabaman lady claimed recently in a moment of indiscretion: 'It's all the fault of the blacks.' 'All' being almost every problem facing the Southern states apart from the threat of a nuclear holocaust. Or, as a deputy sheriff was to declare so revealingly over a drink in a bar in a Mississippi town: 'Damn niggers. Squatting in the fields propagating themselves.'

Integration may be the official policy, but towns and cities are still divided, with blacks living on the whole in the poor sections and the whites in the affluent areas. Schools may be desegregated, but blacks and whites are educated mostly in their home areas thus creating racially separated schools. The policy of bussing children to school in other areas has had little effect and has brought about a rise in the number of private schools to serve the demand of white parents who wish, not unnaturally, that their children should have the best education, not that offered by schools in black areas which are often badly equipped and poorly funded.

The civil rights activists may have achieved their aim of desegregating the buses, but take a bus ride into downtown Atlanta, Georgia, for example, and look at the colour of the passengers. They are mostly black. Only the very poor whites use public transport. The bus and metro system in Atlanta is commonly known by its acronym MARTA, which officially stands for Metropolitan Atlanta Rapid Transport Authority. In white circles however they say it means Moving Africans Rapidly Through Atlanta. The modern metro system is one of the few in the country which primarily serves poor, black neighbourhoods. It is one way of keeping black people in their ghettoes and out of the white areas. Cobb County, which borders the city limits with its black population of more than 50 per cent, is 96 per cent white. Only in 1989 did the county authorities reluctantly agree to allow MARTA to cross its borders. This is an area where they do a good line in T-shirts bearing the message: 'Trade with South Africa – our blacks for your whites.'

America may appear to have honoured its black leaders. There are numerous Martin Luther King Jr Boulevards, Streets, Avenues and Bridges named after the great black minister. There is, in Atlanta, at the site of his tomb, a museum dedicated to his memory. But the unwary traveller should be warned that it is situated deep in a run-down black area of the city into which many whites would consider it unwise to wander. The Ku Klux Klan may be less overt about its operations, but it still holds rallies in the South even though on the whole they are poorly attended. More significantly, in the state of Louisana in February 1989, a former Klan leader, a grand wizard no less, was elected to the state legislature in a nearly all-white district of New Orleans despite public opposition from the newly elected President Bush. Black leaders were surprisingly pleased. They were glad that white racism was now out in the open, they said. It is easier to fight it when you can see it.

The standard of living for the average black family has shown no great improvement. It even dropped during the final years of President Reagan's administration. Poverty and unemployment is endemic among blacks, and soup kitchens are still to be found in towns and cities. In 1986, according to US Government statistics, almost one in three blacks were considered to be living below the poverty line, compared to about one in ten whites. On a state by state basis, nearly 24 per cent of the total Mississippi population was below the poverty line. In the country as a whole the figure was 11.6 per cent. As is the case in most industrialised societies, crime and the use of drugs seem to go hand in hand with poverty and unemployment. Homicide, it is hard to believe, is the number one cause of death for young black men in the USA. A black male has a 1 in 21 chance of being murdered compared to a 1 in 311 chance for his white counterpart.

Edward's uncle, Nathaniel Lewis, put his finger on it in 1987, shortly before his nephew died, when Clive contacted him during his attempts to stop the execution. 'Back when I was growing up, Leake County had a lot of racial problems. In the next county over is Philadelphia where the three Freedom Fighters were killed. With integration a few things changed on the surface, but nothing changed deep down. There was not much difference between the times when I was coming up and when Edward Earl was.' Lawyer Jess Brown believes so too. 'Things have improved in Mississippi since the civil rights years,' he says. 'We have a black federal judge, a black state judge. But how people feel does not change. Things do not improve on the ground.'

Their views are backed up by a Leake County black woman who has better cause to know the realities of the situation in the Walnut Grove area than almost anyone else. Winson Hudson has been president of the Leake County chapter of the NAACP for 28 years. She is the co-chairman of the Democratic Party for Leake County, the first black woman to hold that position. She has also served on the Mississippi state executive committee of the Democratic Party, working towards the integration of the party. In 1989 she was among 75 black women whose lives were portrayed in a major national exhibition. The women were chosen because in one way or another they have helped to change American society. Winson Hudson, now 73 years old, has lived through the years of segregation, the struggle for black emancipation and the times that have followed. Her own family suffered at the hands of the whites. When she was a baby her uncle was lynched without trial for a minor offence against a white man. She came to know Edward as a little boy when she was responsible for organising a black self-help project known as Head Start, a product of Freedom

Summer. The scheme was designed to provide pre-school children with a sound basis for their further education. Edward was one of the children who benefitted from this programme.

'It was very hard back then to get a programme such as Head Start off the ground,' said Winson in a statement she provided about Edward's background, used by Clive during his last-minute appeals to save the life of the young black man. 'There was opposition to the programme on the part of the white residents of the community. Also many of the black residents, whose children stood to be the principal beneficiaries of the programme, were afraid to become involved. Back up in communities like Walnut Grove, it was very scary. By that I mean that the people up in that community, the black people, were scared to get involved.' Edward's grandfather, Phinas, however, was not one to be frightened off. He was an outspoken man and an active member of the local NAACP, unlike his wife who kept her head down and contented herself with the family, home and church. 'Many of the black people in the area would be willing to contribute money to the NAACP but they were afraid and they would tell you that they didn't want their names on any list or did not want to sign anything,' says Winson Hudson. Phinas Lewis was one of the exceptions and gave his open backing to the organisation.

Winson Hudson believes, in common with many others, that Edward was wrongly convicted of the Walnut Grove murder. It is a belief based on a close knowledge of Edward who she knew to be a quiet and well-behaved boy, and on the evidence – or lack of it. It is also based on many years of experience in the conduct of law officers and courts in the area, experience that has shown time and again that there are two types of justice in the Southern states, one for whites and one for blacks. 'The law was against him from the start. That was the problem. Nothing else mattered because the law was against him,' she says. Was Edward unlucky to be in the wrong place at the wrong time? 'Oh yes,' says Winson Hudson with feeling. 'He was unlucky. He was unlucky to be born black.' And she, too, feels that a similar miscarriage of justice could happen again. 'Things have changed some,' she says, 'but sure, it could happen again.'

Winson Hudson can draw support for some of her views from a seemingly surprising source. She is black, but Justice James Robertson is white, a Mississippi version of former President Jimmy Carter in appearance. He sits on the Mississippi Supreme Court, the highest court in the state. In the eyes of his electors his credentials for the post are good. Firstly, he is Mississippi born and bred, down to his open-neck checked shirt and casual denims. His appearance suggests he is more likely to be off for a day's hunting in the woods, like so many of his fellow Mississippians, than administering justice in the state's top court. But there is something that separates him from his colleagues on the Supreme Court. He is a Harvard educated man, and unlike them, knows something of life outside Mississippi and the Southern states. He is the only judge on the Supreme Court to have been educated outside the state. He is intelligent and well-educated with a broader view of the world than it is possible for those to obtain who have never left the narrow confines of Mississippi.

These factors help to explain some of the differences that exist between him and his colleagues. Justice Robertson is opposed to the death penalty, and on the Supreme Court he stands alone on that. He also admits that there is still a difference in the way justice is administered for blacks and whites, although his views are understandably more circumspect than those of Winson Hudson. 'There is still a racial component in the way the law is handled. There is no question about it,' he confirmed, sitting behind an imposing desk in his Supreme Court office. 'It is not as strong as it used to be, but it is there.'

Justice Robertson also knew Edward Johnson. He represented him at his first appeal in 1982 when he was still an attorney in private practice. So did the state execute an innocent man? 'No,' says Justice Robertson. 'It did not. Edward Johnson was guilty. He was identified by one of the witnesses.' It is a weak argument, as the witness changed her story several times, but Justice Robertson is an upholder of the law and must be seen to be so. Nevertheless it was a bad night for him on May 20th, 1987, the night Edward died. 'People here believe in Old Testament vengeance,' he says. 'It is an eye for an eye, a tooth for a tooth.'

Christianity in the Deep South is a force to be reckoned with. A visitor to the area, who wishes to remain popular with the local people, is advised to answer 'Yes' if asked if he is a member of the faith. The next question will then be: 'Which church do you attend?' There are many different Christian sects flourishing in the Deep South, but the largest and most influential is the Southern Baptists. They take their Old Testament literally. The average Mississippi family income is the lowest in the nation but this poverty is not evident from the affluent appearance of the proliferation of churches in the state. The main Southern Baptist church in the capital city of Jackson occupies several blocks. Its offices stretch for several hundred yards. The prosperous air of the churches is shared by only two other categories of buildings in the state – banks and government offices. Christianity is a part of the social fabric. In contrast to the situation in Britain, most ministers can rely on a full house on Sundays. In areas like Leake County the message of the churches spills out onto the roadside in a multitude of hand-painted signs exhorting drivers to obey the word of the Lord. 'Sin not, abstain from evil, serve the Lord,' they proclaim. Some have an unwitting comic touch: 'Sebastapol – the home of God's Love Letters' declares the sign outside the small town where Edward Johnson used to work. Others are less amusing. 'Thou shalt not steal; thou shall not commit adultery,' reads another. The exhortation 'Thou shalt not kill' is noticeably lacking.

Religion and the concept of justice are closely intertwined in the South. Clive Stafford Smith recounts the story of the day, shortly after joining the Southern Prisoners' Defence Committee, when he was in a rural Georgian court defending a client accused of murder. As was his right, he was quizzing those called to sit on the jury about their views on the death penalty. 'Ah'm in favour of it for everything the Bible says,' said one elderly white woman. Whereupon Clive took up a copy of the Bible, without which no self-respecting lawyer would enter a Southern court-room, and asked her whether she was familiar with Numbers, chapter 15, verse 34. When she replied she was not, he asked her to read the verse which recounts an incident where a man was stoned to death for collecting firewood on the Sabbath. 'Are you in favour of the death penalty for any-one who picks up sticks on Sunday?' he asked her triumphantly, feeling secure in the response he would receive. There was a long pause. Then the woman replied: 'Well, it's there, so ah s'pose ah'd have to be, wouldn't ah?' The woman was allowed to sit on the jury trying a man for murder.

The denomination which tends to have among its followers those of a more liberal persuasion is the Episcopalian Church, closely connected to the Anglican Church in England. The Reverend Colton Smith is assistant to the Episcopalian Bishop of Mississippi. His roots are firmly founded in the state, stretching back into the Civil War years. But he received a part of his education in New York City, is married to an Englishwoman and has spent many months in England where he established close links with Coventry Cathedral and its mission of reconciliation. Colton Smith is one of those few Mississippians who can view his homeland with the eyes of an outsider. 'Most people here think in terms of retribution when it comes to punishment,' he said, citing again the examples laid down in the Old Testament. He, too, is an exception in that he is opposed to the death penalty, but he is not optimistic about changes in the future. 'There is a frontier spirit here,' he said. 'Life is cheap. People are measured by their productivity. If they are poor and not working, as is the case with many blacks, they are not worth much. Things have progressed a little racially since the 1960s, but many people have been left behind. It will take decades, hundreds of years, to change people's attitudes. The fact that there is now a Death Row and black people are tried by juries is an advance, a move forward. Before that they were just lynched without trial.' Depressing words. He does not advise outsiders to probe too deeply into Deep South attitudes and opinions. Southerners have a defensive spirit, he explains, resulting from more than 100 years of being the underdog. Unlike the rest of the USA they know from the Civil War what it is like to lose. Losing in Vietnam is the closest the rest of the country has come to experiencing that situation. 'Southern hospitality is skin deep,' he warns. 'Just do not ask any serious questions and you will be OK. People do not want to hear from you if you have different opinions.'

The Southern white is an enigma, as much to his Northern cousins as a true foreigner. We are all outsiders. There is a joke told in the North that goes like this: A Northern woman is stopped on the highway by a Southern cop. She asks to know what offence she has committed. The cop, hearing her Northern accent, demands: 'Where y'all from then?' 'I'm from the planet earth,' replies the woman scathingly. 'Where are you from?' Jokes have a way of getting to the heart of things.

The music of a land is also often revealing about the people who live there. In the American Deep South they love their country and western songs. The bars are full of tough-looking, checked-shirted men clutching their tight-lipped women with their outdated coiffured hair-dos to their chests as they meander over the dance floor to the strains of a sad and sentimental ballad. The lyrics tell of misery and despair, of lost love, bereavement, poverty and hard times. It is as though melancholia were a national disease. Songs such as 'A Tear in my Beer', a hit in 1989, are improbable favourites in a place where men are men and would be no more likely to weep than take up embroidery for a hobby. Could it be that even hard-bitten, defensive Southern whites have a need to reveal a softer underbelly? The singer of 'A Tear in my Beer' is Hank Williams Jr, from Jackson, Mississippi, a true red-neck according to a couple of fans from South Carolina, who have no reservations about the pot calling the kettle black. Backwoodsman he may be, but he has captured the essence of the South in another of his songs. It reflects simply but effectively the divisions that dominate the attitudes of people in the Deep South. Some of the words go like this:

> 'The city is against the county,
> The county is against the state,

> The state is against the government
> And the highway still ain't paved.
> The banker's against the farmer,
> The farmer's against the wall,
> The doctor's against me smoking
> And the devil's against us all.
> The cops are against the robbers,
> The laws are against the cops
> Justice is against the system
> And some people are blowing their tops.'

This then, is the Deep South in which Edward grew up. This is the society into which he was born and which nineteen years later condemned him to die. It is a divided, racially segregated, backward, bigoted world. As a poor, Southern black he had little chance of a good life. As it was, he was never to be given any chance at all.

*   *   *

Most of the population of Walnut Grove were asleep in bed the night that town marshal Jake Trest was gunned down in the main street as he was on his way to investigate a disturbance. It was a hot and steamy June night in 1979, typical of the summer months in Mississippi when the midday humidity reaches such heights that the least movement drenches people in sweat. The air vibrated to the interminable rasping of the crickets, an ever-present background drone from which there is no escape. In their beds the inhabitants of the town tossed fitfully in the heat.

Jake Trest was 42 and had been a marshal for a mere two months. A veteran of the Korean War, he had been through a succession of jobs before taking up his brother Herbert's suggestion that he should join him as the second of two marshals in the small community. The job did not pay well, but neither did it demand much. Keeping a night-time watch on the orderly little community seemed ideal for a man who wanted a quiet life. That Friday night he had started his shift as usual at about 11.00 pm, taking over from Herbert. The two exchanged a few words but there was nothing much to report. All seemed peaceful in Walnut Grove.

But, some time after 2.00 am, Jake was alerted to the first signs of trouble. Precisely what it was that aroused his suspicions may never be known, but it is probable that he left his office to cast his eye over the sleeping town and noticed something amiss at a house a couple of hundred yards down the road, the home of a 69-year-old white woman, a widow called Sally Franklin, who lived alone apart from her long-term lodger. He may have seen a black man enter her home, which would have been unusual in any circumstances. He may only have noticed a car parked outside that had not been there before. Whatever it was, it was enough to make the marshal decide it warranted a closer look. Armed with a powerful .357 calibre Smith & Wesson revolver he got into his patrol car and drove the short distance down the road to investigate. He drew to a halt about fifteen yards away from the house and seems to have left the vehicle in a hurry for it was found later parked at an angle to the kerb with headlights on and the driver's door open.

But Jake Trest never arrived at Sally Franklin's door. His body was found shortly afterwards lying in a pool of blood in front of his car. He had been shot five times at point-blank range, twice in the head with bullets from his own gun and three times in the body with a light-weight pistol. A graphic description of the dead man was to be given in court by Dr David Moody, the doctor who was called to the scene of the crime. 'Mr Trest was lying in a prone position, face down, right side of his face down, with a large amount of blood extruded on to the ground around his body ... He was found to have numerous wounds to his body, the first of which was what appeared to be a burst type injury to the left forehead. This was a gaping wound that was as if it had been done with a blunt instrument. On the chest there were three entrance wounds, what appeared to be small calibre bullets.' The doctor then went on to describe the two head wounds. 'There was brain tissue, cerebral spine fluid, a large amount of blood extruding from the right ear at that time. There was blood, mainly all over his torso and shirt, both his shirts, his undershirt, from the numerous wounds.'

The sound of the shots ringing through the night awakened nearby residents. Others were alerted by a phone call from Sally Franklin's house. They found the old lady, battered, bruised and in a state of shock on the floor of her kitchen. They also discovered the body of the town marshal. A call was made to the sheriff's department in the nearby town of Carthage, the centre of Leake County administration. Walnut Grove mayor Bob Dawson arrived quickly on the scene, followed shortly afterwards by the head of the local police, Sheriff Joe Mack Thaggard, along with fellow law officers. There was no sign of the assailant.

Miss Sally, as she is known in the area, stammered out her story of what had happened that night. She had been asleep in bed, she said, when she was woken by a knock at the back door in the early hours of the morning. On going to investigate she found a young black man at the door. He told

Miss Sally, who earned extra money by selling Avon cosmetics, that he had come to pay off a cosmetics bill owed by his sister. Miss Sally did not open the door but accepted the money proffered through the window and went to get some change. When she returned the man said he also wanted a bottle of perfume for his sister. Again Miss Sally left the door and went to find the order. As she was searching her cupboards, she was alarmed to hear the sound of the insect screen being torn from the door. She ran back to find the black man had forced his way into the house. 'He grabbed me by the arm and he hit me on the head,' Miss Sally testified at the trial. 'He said: "I come in here to get me some pussy. I want pussy." Well, man, I fought until I thought I would die, and he kept just pushing me and pushing me and got me in the back room and I told him, I says: "If you won't kill me, I've got a lot of money hid. I will give it to you." And when I said that he pushed me and slammed me and I run, and he realised I was running from him. Run up the hall about six feet through the kitchen, across the den, and he caught me from behind with them big hands.' And that, said Miss Sally, was the last she remembered before she lost consciousness. The commotion had woken the lodger, a Mr Carmen Dennis. He was far from being a well man and died shortly before the trial. Nevertheless, weak and sick though he was, he left his bed to find out the cause of the disturbance. The intruder fled as he came into the room. At this moment Marshal Trest was approaching the house in his car. There are no witnesses to what happened next. But it is assumed the marshal leaped from his car when he saw the fleeing man and was killed as he tried to apprehend him.

This is the story that Sheriff Joe Mack Thaggard says he heard when he arrived in Walnut Grove about 30 minutes later. This is the story as told to the rest of the world. It appeared that there was a vicious criminal at large, a man who would stop at nothing. A black man who would break into the house of an elderly white woman, threaten to rape her, beat her senseless and pump five bullets into the body of a town marshal in an attempt to escape. The sheriff immediately decided to call in all his resources to track down this murderous individual. Deputy sheriffs and highway patrol investigators throughout the county were alerted by radio and telephone and headed for Walnut Grove. The hunt for the killer was on.

Edward Johnson was tinkering with his beaten-up old Buick car on the dirt road leading to his grandmother's home when a police car pulled up beside him at about 2.00 pm on that Saturday afternoon. There were two men in the car, deputy sheriff Jimmy Callahan, who was white, and deputy sheriff Terry Truss, a black man. They told Edward they wanted to take him into Walnut Grove for questioning in connection with the murder. Edward was not the first young black to be picked up by the cops in the area that day, nor was he the last. The police had little to go on. Miss Sally had been unable to identify her attacker and could only provide a vague description that could have fitted any number of young blacks. In such cases, although the police are loath to admit it, their policy is to round up any black who might fit the bill, fingerprint them, interrogate them and hope that enough evidence can be found to make a charge against one of them. Edward was the third young man to be picked up by those two policemen that day. Other officers were doing likewise throughout the area.

The deputy sheriffs took Edward to Miss Sally's house. They wanted to discover, they said, whether he was of a similar height to the man described by the old lady by measuring him against her back door. It was to be a matter of dispute at Edward's trial whether or not Miss Sally saw him when he was brought to the house. His defence lawyers were to claim that she did, that Edward was taken into the house and that Miss Sally then told the police that he was not her attacker. The prosecution claimed that Edward remained outside and was never in Miss Sally's presence. Be that as it may, Edward was subsequently allowed home after being taken to the City Hall for fingerprinting.

The following day Edward was questioned once again at Walnut Grove City Hall. How he came to be there is again a matter of dispute. Edward and his relatives say that he was sitting in the shade of a tree outside his grandmother's home when the sheriff drove up and told the youth to accompany him into the town for more questioning. The official story, unlikely though it may seem, is that Edward simply turned up at the City Hall that Sunday afternoon, no-one is quite sure how or why. The point was crucial to both the prosecution and the defence in the subsequent trial as the police had to show that Edward had not been illegally detained before he was finally arrested and charged. The defence were eager to show the reverse and thus convince the judge that evidence obtained from these interrogations was inadmissable.

There is no dispute, however, about the fact that while at the City Hall Edward was told he would have to go to the Mississippi state capital of Jackson for a lie detector test that very afternoon. He was taken to a waiting patrol car and with Joe Mack in the front passenger seat, Mississippi Highway Patrol investigator Rudolph Adcock driving and Edward in the rear, they set off on the 50-mile trip. It must have been a terrifying experience for the young black man. Edward was eighteen years old, and had never been in trouble with the law before. He had had no experience of dealing with police officers. He had not spoken to a lawyer, nor had it been suggested that he should or could do so. He was so ignorant about what was involved in taking a polygraph test he thought it might hurt. He was black, alone in the car with two white, burly, armed officers looking to pin a murder charge on him. He was a very frighened boy.

The lawmen and their suspect never reached Jackson. Shortly after turning on to the main highway Edward announced he would like to make a statement. A tape recorder was switched on. He then, completely voluntarily and without any pressure, confessed to the murder of Jake Trest and the attack on Sally Franklin. Or at least, that is the sheriff's story. Edward on the other hand said he admitted to the crimes because he feared for his life if he did not do so. Whatever the truth of the matter, and it was to be hotly debated in court, there was no longer any cause for the three men to continue to Jackson.

The sheriff now had what he needed. He had set off for Jackson with no evidence at all which could be used against Edward. He now had a full and total confession. The youth was taken to the court house in Carthage where the sheriff wrote down the confession and Edward signed it. He was officially placed under arrest and charged with murder. The sheriff was well pleased. This had looked like a tough investigation and he had cracked it in less than two days. The dangerous killer was now safely behind bars where he could do no further harm to the innocent population. It was perhaps surprising that he should turn out to be an eighteen-year-old youth without a stain on his character, known throughout the area as a quiet, hard-working boy. But the sheriff was not going to lose any sleep over minor matters like that. For him it had been a good weekend's work. There were a few loose ends to be tidied up but there was nothing the sheriff could not handle. It was an open and shut case. Edward was as good as dead.

Five

Mississippi Justice

There are, it would be agreed by seekers after truth, many questions that people in Walnut Grove in June 1979 might have asked themselves about the weekend's activities had they chosen to do so. There are aspects of the story which did not seem to hang together, that might have caused observers some nagging doubts if they had wanted to look more closely.

Why, for example, did the investigators of the crime have to take Edward to Miss Sally's house to judge his height and thereby risk a vital witness being prejudiced by the sight of a possible suspect? Why not simply use a tape measure? Why, if this violent criminal was armed with a gun, did he not use it to threaten or even kill Miss Sally? Was it not strange that a desperado such as this would be calmly sitting under a tree or tinkering with his car when the hunt was on? He must be a very cool customer. Was it not odd that a black man should come to Miss Sally's door in the early hours of the morning to pay a cosmetics bill? Did she not think it was very odd? Could it be that her story was less than honest?

And what of Edward? Did he fit the bill as murderer and potential rapist? According to many who knew him, whites as well as blacks, he did not. He was known throughout the area as a quiet young man, almost old-fashioned in his behaviour, a hard worker who had succeeded, without excelling himself, in graduating from high school. At the time of the murder he had a job at a chicken processing plant in the nearby town of Seabastapol, and was regarded as a reliable employee. Socially he was relatively restrained for a teenager. He was known to drink fairly heavily on occasion, mostly beer, but did not take drugs as many youngsters did. He had a girlfriend in nearby Philadelphia and his usual weekend activities revolved around driving over to see her or playing cards with friends and relatives in the Walnut Grove area. He was proud of the old

61

car, which he had bought with his hard-earned savings. People knew him to be unaggressive to a fault. At school he had avoided fights and had to be encouraged to stick up for himself rather than the reverse.

Jessie Mae could pride herself on the way she had brought Edward up. All his relatives thought well of him, including those living in Chicago whom he used to visit regularly during the school summer holidays. Many of them gave glowing reports to Clive during the last three weeks of Edward's life when, for the benefit of the appeal courts, he questioned them about their young relative in an attempt to build up a picture of the man scheduled to die. They loved Edward, they said. He was a sensitive, well-mannered boy. A great uncle, Cornelius Lewis, told Clive: 'When Edward Earl stayed at our house those two summers, when he was sixteen or seventeen, he was very good. He would pitch in and help around the house and carried his weight with things that needed to be done. He never was any kind of behaviour problem. He never went out a lot at night. He would mostly stay around the family. He never would sulk or get aggravated or withdrawn, like some teenagers do. He was always very open and friendly. He was not hostile and did not fight with the other kids.'

This opinion was supported by Samuel Hoye, the principal of South Leake High School, where Edward was a pupil. 'Edward Earl had a good relationship with his peers,' he said. 'He was a well-liked young man. In fact he was probably one of the most liked students we had here at South Leake. He was one of those boys that people remember the good things that he did. He was not a young man to cause any kind of disturbance and in fact he didn't cause any disturbance on campus. Edward Earl was an obedient, well-mannered person. As far as Edward Earl's moral values and sense of right and wrong, he got these from his grandmother. She was the type of woman who did not believe in sparing the rod and spoiling the child. She believed that they were never too old to take a switch to them as long as they lived under her roof. Edward Earl feared his grandmother, but it was a fear born out of respect and he would never do anything knowingly that he felt she would disapprove of.' Edward was in fact devoted to Jessie Mae and, apart from his visits to relatives in the North, never stayed away from the house at night.

His aunt, Thelma Johnson, who lived next door echoed the feelings of many when she told Clive: 'When the trouble came in 1979, no-one I knew could believe that Edward Earl could have done what he was charged with doing.' Respectful, kind and considerate were the words most people used to describe the young man. 'It is very difficult for me to believe that Edward Earl could be executed for the death of a policeman,' his uncle, Nathaniel Lewis, was to say many years later. 'There is too much goodness in him.' Another relative, Lillie Randall, the pastor of a Chicago church, was shocked to hear what had happened to her cousin. 'As a child he was such a quiet person and seemed like a homely type,' she said. 'He was never a violent person during the time I was round him. He had very good manners and treated his elders with respect.' The list of people who volunteered to testify to Edward's good character is long. Were they all so very wrong? Could this quiet, well-behaved young man have gone out that night to rape and murder and then calmly return home to his grandmother?

But at the time of the murder, no-one in Walnut Grove asked these questions. Or at least no-one of any importance did. No-one white. Edward was safely locked up inside Leake County jail in Carthage. Who cared about unanswered questions? He was only a poor black anyway.

Some people did care, however. Edward's family cared very much indeed. His grandmother had done her utmost over the Saturday and Sunday to look after the young man's interests but it was an unequal fight. When Edward was first picked up on the Saturday she had paid her neighbour to drive her into Walnut Grove and had followed the police car to Miss Sally's house. She knew the white woman well, having been employed as a domestic servant by her in the past, and had gone into the house to discover what was happening to her grandson. That scene among others was to be replayed at the trial. On the Sunday, she had again followed Edward and the sheriff into Walnut Grove, this time with her daughter Thelma, in an attempt to be present with her grandson at the City Hall. But the two women were refused admittance. Jessie Mae also asked to go with Edward to Jackson when he was taken away for the lie detector test, but again she was ordered away. Later that night she heard her grandson had been arrested and charged with murder. She immediately went to see him in Carthage jail and they were allowed a few minutes together during which Edward told her what she was already certain of – that he was innocent.

At this stage Edward had had no communication with a lawyer and it was to be some time before he did. His family were to encounter great difficulties finding a lawyer willing to act for him. There was no-one in the area prepared to take on the job. The attorneys in Leake County were all white and had no interest in defending a black man charged with murdering a white policeman, even if the family could have afforded to pay their bills. Emotions in the county were running high among the white population. It was more than any lawyer's job or life was worth to associate himself in any way with the man who most of the white community were already convinced was the perpetrator of this terrible crime.

In desperation the family turned to the only man they knew of who might be able to save Edward. Back in the 1960s, in that area of Mississippi, there had been a black lawyer working in the civil rights movement who had become something of a local hero. Jess Brown was an old man now, 67 years old and in poor health, but he was still alive and practising law in the city of Jackson. He was asked if he would come to Edward's defence. Even he was not immediately anxious to do so. Representing a man charged with capital murder in a case such as this would be an emotionally and mentally demanding task and Jess no longer felt he had the stamina to cope with it. He was ill-prepared to handle the case having had no recent experience of capital murder charges. Since he was based in Jackson and there was no way either he or Edward's family could afford to pay his expenses to stay in the area, he would be required to make a daily round trip of more than 100 miles simply to be present in court. He had no local knowledge of the people who were to be involved in the trial, which was to put him at a disadvantage against the prosecution. There were numerous reasons why he should not become involved in this particular case. But to his credit he did eventually agree to take it on. During the ensuing trial it would be easy to criticise him for his inefficient and sometimes inept handling of the procedure, and Clive Stafford Smith was much later to claim the incompetence of Edward's trial lawyers as a cause for overturning the death sentence imposed. It was an action that Clive was reluctant to take as he respected Jess for his role during the civil rights years; but it was also an action that Jess himself cooperated in, because he viewed saving Edward's life as more important than his own professional pride. It is also important to remember that at that time, in 1979, it was Jess, and only Jess, who answered the family's cry for help.

It was unfortunate to say the least that there was another crucial factor which would handicap Jess Brown in his handling of the case. He had become deaf in his old age, very deaf, which was to lead to situations in court that would have been farcical if they had not been so serious. During the questioning of one of the witnesses by the prosecution, for example, the following dialogue takes place:

'*Brown*:   Could I say this, your Honour, for the record? That ...
Judge: Are you making an objection or anything?

Clive Stafford Smith

The gas chamber at Parchman Penitentiary, Mississippi

Edward Johnson with his grandmother, Jessie Mae, shortly before he died. As a special privilege, relatives are not confined to the barred visiting area for their last visit before the execution

A typical pawn shop in Leake County, Mississippi

Jessie Mae's home near Walnut Grove where Edward was brought up

Brown: Sir?

Judge: Are you making an objection?

Brown: Yes sir. I . . . well, I am just objecting to the witness continuing arguing and badgering the witness.

Judge: I have already ruled. You just didn't hear me, Jess.

Brown: Oh, I'm sorry.'

On the last day of the trial the point is made even more pertinently by the judge. The defence is arguing that some of the jurors cannot read or write and are therefore not fit to sit on a jury. The judge has the following comment to make:

'*Judge*:   I think we could go into a hearing on R. Jess Brown. He can't hear. So that goes into his ability as a trial attorney.

Brown: Sir? I heard my name.

Judge: We're talking about you, Jess.'

The lawyer's hearing disability was so great that almost all the questioning of witnesses in court was undertaken by his junior partner on the case, a young black attorney by the name of Firnist Alexander. He was a bright young man who was to make some telling points during cross-examination, but he had very little experience of criminal cases of any type, and had never before been involved in a capital murder charge. Clive was to claim in last-minute appeals to stop Edward's execution in 1987 that between them the two attorneys had made many errors in their understanding of the law and failed to represent Edward effectively at his trial. At that time in 1979, however, just after Edward's arrest, the family was not in a position to pick and choose a legal adviser. They were just grateful that someone, anyone, was going to try and help. Their worries were compounded by the fact that they did not know how they were going to pay the costs involved. Here they were helped by the local NAACP and its leader Winson Hudson, who organised a fund-raising drive throughout the black community in the area to raise money to pay Edward's legal fees. Even so, Jess Brown never received the full sum, meagre though it was, for which he had agreed to take on the case.

Edward was first brought before a court on July 2nd, a month after his arrest, for a *habeas* hearing called to establish that the state had enough evidence to justify proceeding with the prosecution. The judge, the Honourable Marcus D Gordon, of the Eight Circuit Court, ruled that there was a case to be answered. This man was to top the bill of *dramatis personae* when Edward's trial eventually began in the August of the following year in the small Leake County courthouse in Carthage.

Judges in the United States as in Britain are well known for their idiosyncratic and eccentric ways. Many seem happy to encourage the blurring of the distinction between courtroom and theatre. They do not necessarily write the lines, they do not always have a starring role, but theirs is the dominant influence. Marcus Gordon was no exception. Just as a director leaves his mark upon the interpretation of a play, Gordon's personality was to be the major factor in the creation of the atmosphere in the Leake County courtroom when Edward was brought to trial. He was to direct the course of the case not simply in legal terms but through the strength of his beliefs and character. He ran his court with that deceptively casual air commonly depicted in bar scenes in Western movies, when the underlying tension is revealed only when a wrong move is made and people reach for their guns.

Marcus Gordon was a man who had done well for himself. A family man who now lived in the small town of Union in neighbouring Newton County, he had been born and raised in Leake County itself. He was a native Mississippian who had come a long way, the first in his family to have received an education, his father having left school at a young age. He had worked hard to get where he was and believed in making others do likewise, while at the same time maintaining a relaxed and informal manner. In essence he seemed to be a kind and considerate man, but his easy-going manner would at times seem grotesquely at odds with the life and death issue with which he was dealing. Not that Marcus Gordon was probably aware of his jarring tone.

He showed great concern for the well-being of the jury. During the first day of the trial he interrupted the evidence of one of the witnesses to ask of the jury: 'Do any of the jurors smoke? You may smoke if you would like. Do you have an ashtray? Get the juror an ashtray. Have y'all had any coffee since you have been here this morning?'

He could not have been more solicitous if he had been entertaining them in his own home. 'I want you to be as comfortable as I can make you,' he tells the jury that same day. 'I want you also to relax and enjoy yourselves while you are serving as jurors.'

Gordon continued this tone throughout the trial. On the final day of the trial after the jury had found Edward guilty of murder, Marcus Gordon thought it fitting to discuss the merits of various hotels. 'Good morning,' he greets the jury. 'You look as fresh as you did last Monday to me. Well, you will have to concede it is not every jury that gets to stay in the Ramada Inn. They treat you real nice down there, don't they?' This to a jury that had reassembled as required under American law to decide on the appropriate sentence for the crime, whether Edward should live or die.

The judge's courteous manner with the jury extended itself to the prosecution witnesses and lawyers where first-name terms were commonly in use. When Sally Franklin was on the witness stand Marcus Gordon referred to her as 'Miss Sally', the name by which she was known by her friends and acquaintances. She at times called the judge 'Marcus'. At one point Marcus Gordon stopped the cross-examination of Miss Sally because of his concern that continued questioning might adversely affect the health of the old lady.

Marcus Gordon's kindly manner was not so evident in his dealings with the defence lawyers. Both attorneys were apprehensive about the treatment they would receive from the local community, acting as they did on behalf of a black man accused of murdering a white policeman. For Jess Brown, in particular, with his still vivid memories of the civil rights years and his leading role in the struggle, the next few days were to prove especially stressful and intimidating.

For the most part, Marcus Gordon treated the two attorneys with great courtesy. But he was anxious that the proceedings should be conducted as quickly as possible and demonstrated the tougher side of his character when it appeared that Alexander was prepared to dispute one of his rulings, ordering that the sheriff be brought into the courtroom to give added authority. This was the dialogue that took place.

'*Alexander*:	Your Honour, I am trying to find out …
Judge:	Mr Alexander, I have just ruled now.
Alexander:	May I inquire, Your Honour, if I may be permitted to …
Judge:	I am going to …
Alexander:	… ask this witness …
Judge:	… pass another sentence if you don't move on.
Alexander:	Your Honour, I don't know …
Judge:	Call the sheriff in here. I don't want to hear any more. I have ruled.
	(Sheriff Joe Mack Thaggard comes into the courtroom)
Judge:	Are you ready to proceed?
Alexander:	Your Honour, I am ready to proceed, but I don't know what is permissible and what's not, based on what the Court said.

Judge: I am not going to permit you to read that entire record into
                this record. If you have any specific questions, you ask them
                at this time.

Alexander: I may not refer to the transcript any further?

Judge: Sheriff, come around. Are you ready to proceed?

Alexander: Yes, sir.'

In all fairness to the judge, it is not surprising if he at times let his
emotions get the better of him. Marcus Gordon was working under
extremely difficult conditions. He had been placed in a position which
forced him to hear the most serious of trials, a capital murder case, in an
impossibly short space of time. As a circuit judge he had to keep to a
previously laid-down timetable which took him from county courtroom to
county courtroom and did not allow for major trials over-running their
time limit. He was required to hear every case from a speeding ticket to
murder. He had been obliged to convene a special court session in Leake
County in order to fit Edward's case into his schedule at all, and he had
a mere seven days in which to see it through to an end.

He had set a punishing pace. In order to have any hope of seeing the case
through in the allotted number of days he had opened the court session at
8.00 in the morning and kept going sometimes until 10.00 at night with
only a 30-minute recess for lunch. During the period of the trial, 2,000
pages of testimony were taken. 'This lady here is worn to a frazzle,' said
the judge on the last day, referring to the official court reporter. So too was
everyone else. On the third day he had only ended the session at 10.00 pm
on the request of Jess Brown, who found the pace more than he could
bear. Jess argued that keeping the court sitting so late rendered Edward's
defence attorneys ineffective. Marcus Gordon had it placed on the court
record that Jess had requested an adjournment because he did not have
'the strength of body of someone younger'. He was at pains to note that
several of the jurors appeared to be older than Jess and that although the
two defence attorneys also faced a 50-mile drive to and from Jackson, they
were not the only ones to suffer. 'I live in Union, which is approximately
50 miles from here,' he said. 'I drive approximately the same distance that
anyone else would drive. The court reporter, in addition lives in Rankin
County, Brandon, which is approximately 65 miles. So we all have
problems.'

'I have tried to push the attorneys into getting to the meat and the
coconut of their cases, both the state and the defendant,' the judge
continued. 'A circuit judge is nothing more than a sitting duck. Normally,

he sits here, and those things come in, and he lets them go, trying to afford both a fair trial. I have attempted to bring the cases into line, and here we now approach 10.00 o'clock on Wednesday night. Conceivably, we only have three remaining days to conclude a case that I see no end to at this time.'

The following day the judge's patience was pushed beyond endurance when it was discovered that the official indictment against Edward had been incorrectly worded, the date of the murder being put as June 7th rather than June 2nd. The District Attorney asked for it to be amended. Alexander, seeing an opportunity to call for a re-trial, objected. The judge, deprived of the time or necessary tools to reflect on decisions of law, and driven to distraction by the incompetence he was witnessing, made a cry from the heart.

'Only the Good Lord knows what I, as a trial judge, have gone through for a period of time on criminal matters, with indictments needing to be amended to conform to the proof . . . a multitude of problems . . . This trial judge, every opportunity he has ever had to talk to a legislator, has begged for some kind of assistance to the trial judge, in a way of runner, administrator, or someone to assist him in cases of this type and situations of this type, where he is confronted with decisions.

'I do everything that I possibly can in a trial of a case to give an accused a fair trial . . .

'I am only human. It is impossible here four days for me to remember each and every item of testimony, and who testified to what. I just do the very best that I can. I am not a chancery judge where I can take matters under advisement and have the court reporter to type out pertinent portions of testimony, and for me to render a decision some six months later, to have an opportunity to go to some library and sound scholarly and wise and knowledgeable in the law . . .'

How could he be expected to rule correctly in cases like Edward's in such circumstances, Marcus Gordon wanted to know. How could he make legal decisions in a courtroom such as that of Carthage where there were not even any books to which he could refer? 'I am required to make an instant decision on the law,' he said. 'In this county, more particularly than any county in my district, there is not a law library. There is no one place that I can go, if I had the time, to research the law on a given issue of law. The only thing that I have available to me is a Mississippi Code, of which some of the volumes are missing, and the pocket parts are missing and are out of date.'

Providing a judge with a guide to the law was obviously a low priority in Leake County. There is no doubting the sincerity with which the judge spoke.

In accordance with the law of the land, the court was obliged to oversee the selection of twelve men and women, who could be seen to be a representative sample of the young man's peers.

Sixty-three people from Leake County were put forward as possible jurors. Of the twelve who were finally selected after questioning by the judge, prosecution and defence lawyers, only three were black. Nine of the jurors were women. Eight of them lived in Carthage or the surrounding area. Two of the women worked for a shirt-manufacturing company in Walnut Grove itself, and one man was married to a woman who was employed at the same firm. All potential jurors who after questioning expressed any reservations about the imposition of the death penalty were excluded.

There is little remarkable about the composition of this jury when it is compared to many others that are called upon to hear capital murder cases in the American Deep South. Its racial composition might seem unequally balanced with an obvious bias towards white jurors. But there are black prisoners currently on Death Row who have much more cause to claim that the juries which convicted them were racially prejudiced. They were sent to their deaths by all-white juries. More recently the US Supreme Court has ruled that it is unconstitutional for a District Attorney to strike all the black jurors from a jury. But that ruling is not retroactive and did not apply at the time of the Walnut Grove murder trial.

The murder of Marshal Trest was the biggest event to hit this small, close-knit community in living memory. For months, if not years, afterwards, it was a major talking point in the area, widely reported by press and television. As one unusually frank potential juror was to remark in court concerning his knowledge of the murder: 'It's just like anything else, a place this small, a man has twin calves, you will hear about it, whether it is true or not.' This man was not asked to serve.

But in a country where it is usually the jury, not the judge, which decides on the penalty in a capital murder case, the most vital question of all is this. Is a jury, which excludes all those with any reservation about the imposition of the death penalty, a truly representative sample of the accused man's peers? Are not the chosen twelve necessarily biased in favour of sentencing a man to death? It could be that their convictions about the death penalty are so strong they would favour its use in lesser crimes than murder. Shop-lifting, for example. Or for all blacks convicted of any crime. It will never be known how extreme they might have been in their pro-death penalty views since they were never asked. The potential jurors were only asked if they had any qualms or conscientious objections against sentencing a man to death, not if they were rabidly in favour of it. The imbalance seems clear but it does not carry much weight with the men who make the laws in the United States. The issue has been raised before the US Supreme Court in connection with other cases. It has seen fit to rule that it is not unconstitutional to put a man on trial for his life in front of a jury that is totally in favour of executing him should he be found guilty. The ruling does say that people who would automatically impose the death penalty should be excluded from a jury, but it does not mean that any of the twelve chosen would be against it.

After the jury had been sworn in, a further macabre and strange reason for fearing that the twelve men and women would be prejudiced against Edward came to light. On the second day Alexander asked the judge to rule for a mis-trial because the brother of the murdered man, the surviving Walnut Grove marshal, who bore an uncanny resemblance to Jake Trest, was seated in his uniform in the courtroom, a few feet from the jury. Alexander put the point succinctly to the judge. 'In a murder prosecution,' he said, 'generally the victim is not in the courtroom. Now, in this situation, we have got the nearest thing to the victim sitting approximately ten feet from this jury. He is for all practical purposes, symbolically and otherwise, the alter ego of his brother, sitting right here in the courtroom, watching this trial . . . 'Mr Trest has been attired in the uniform of the Walnut Grove town marshal's office, and during his testimony, had previously alluded to the fact that he and his brother shared the same revolver, same equipment, that he had in fact pinned the badge on his brother when he was sworn in as an officer,' Alexander elaborated.

The judge did not agree. 'I will not order this man to leave the courtroom, and I see no prejudicial effect to the man wearing a uniform,' said Marcus Gordon, although he conceded that the marshal was not technically on duty and therefore had no statutory reason for wearing his uniform. The following day, with Herbert Trest back in the same seat, the defence lawyers raised the issue again, this time pointing out that although the marshal had changed into civilian clothes, they were remarkably similar to his uniform. It turned out that the District Attorney had spoken to the marshal and suggested he should change his clothes, a fact which could be interpreted as an acceptance that Alexander had had a valid point.

The judge never addressed the question of whether Herbert Trest's behaviour might influence the jury. The relatives of the murdered man were just as entitled to be present in court as Edward's family, said Marcus Gordon. The marshal had been seated in the same place in his uniform for a whole day before the defence attorneys objected to his presence; therefore they had no right to do so now, he added, not accepting that the only reason Alexander and Brown had not objected earlier was because they had not seen the marshal before, the courtroom being laid out so that the attorneys had their backs to the public area.

If the marshal's presence did influence the jury, it was only of minor importance to the outcome of the case. The result was probably a foregone conclusion from the start. The factors weighing against Edward in the courtroom were so many and varied that it was unlikely he would have been found innocent even if Brown and Alexander had been able to totally demolish the prosecution's evidence. Given the unequal odds, they succeeded remarkably well in highlighting the gaping holes in the testimony of the chief witnesses. But it was a wasted legal exercise.

Six

Confession

Edward was damned by his own words, it was claimed by the prosecution at his trial. He was a self-confessed murderer, a killer who not only admitted he had gunned down Marshal Jake Trest, but was also identified in the courtroom by Miss Sally as the man who had attacked her in her home on the night of the murder. His guilt was incontrovertible. There could be no doubt that this was the man who committed the crimes. The facts were simple, plain for all to see. Edward had confessed and been identified. These, therefore, were the two pillars upon which the prosecution case rested. There was other evidence which would help to point the finger at Edward, but it was of little import compared to the evidence of identification and confession. The District Attorney and his assistant did not, as might be expected, back up their case with a mass of evidence from scientific and forensic experts, probably because they did not have it. They concentrated instead on the two main issues. The defence, for its part, attempted to refute them.

Edward's statement, written down by the sheriff in his Carthage office a few hours after the youngster had confessed all in the police car taking him to Jackson for a lie detector test, read as follows:

'I, Edward Earl Johnson, did on or about the 6th and the 2nd [June 2], 1979 about 2.30 am, stop my car on the street running south beside the Walnut Grove old bank building, or now the drugstore. Was in my 1972 Buick Electra, 225, green in colour. I went up to Sally Franklin's door on the porch. I knocked on the door. She came to the porch and asked me what I wanted. I, Edward Earl Johnson, told her I came to pay Clara Darby's bill. I gave her a $20 bill between the screen and the window facing and told her Clara owed her $10.95. She went and got

73

$9.00 and gave it back through the window to me. At this time, I told her Clara wanted some more perfume, and when she went back in the room for the perfume, I went in the window after I took the screen off over the sink. I met her in the hallway as she was coming back. I hit her and knocked her down on the floor and we fought on the floor. I, Edward Johnson, said give me my money back. She said take it, I got a lot of money, you can have it all. I let her go, and she ran through the kitchen and living room and into the dining room. I, Edward Johnson, caught her. She was trying to holler. I put my hands over her mouth and was holding her. A man came out of the door from another room and hollered at me. I ran to the back door. Tried to open it and could not and jumped through the screen on the back door, went out on the porch and ran over some chairs and fell off on the ground and turned over the wheelbarrow. I, Edward Johnson, left Sally Franklin's house and ran east toward the street. When I got to the street, I turned south and got in my car beside the old bank building, now the drugstore. The police came around the corner of the old bank building from the south in a police car. He stopped and opened the door of the police car and started to get out. He said, 'What are you doing, bud?' I said nothing. At the time I said that, I reach over and got my gun out of the car pocket and put a shell in the barrel. Then the police shined his light in my car. I then jumped out of my car and I shot him two times with my .25 automatic. I was about four foot from him. He slowly fell to the ground off his car fender. He was moving on the ground and moaning. I, Edward Johnson, grabbed his gun. Also, before he fell to the ground, I hit him in the forehead with my gun, and my gun flew out of my hand, and then I grabbed the policeman's gun and shot him two times in the head. I left the policeman lying on the ground in front of his car with the motor running and his lights on. I then jumped in my car and went south, then west, then back north. Then I turned east by Mr Sones' station and went back to the street where Sally Franklin's house was on. I then turned south and went back to where I killed the policeman. I got out and looked around for my gun, a .25 automatic with brown handles. I could not find the gun, so I left and went toward Old Walnut Grove. Just before I got to Old Walnut Grove, my car quit. I got out and threw the policeman's gun out on the west of the road. I was going north toward Old Walnut Grove. I think the policeman's gun was a .357 Magnum. It was a black looking gun. This was on the 6th and 2nd of 1979, on Saturday morning.'

*   *   *

Edward signed this confession in the presence of three police officers in the sheriff's office in Carthage the day after the murder. The officers present were Sheriff Joe Mack Thaggard and Mississippi Highway Patrol investigator Rudolph Adcock, both of whom were in the car when Edward is claimed to have made his verbal confession, and John Coleman, also a criminal investigator with the Mississippi Highway Patrol. All three men were armed, all three had been in the police force for many years, serving as law officers since the civil rights years of the 1960s.

Does it, Alexander asked during his cross-examination of Adcock in court, take three armed, experienced law enforcement officers to take a statement from an eighteen-year-old youth? Adcock was at a loss to explain the presence of the three men. He and the sheriff, he told the court, were there to witness the statement and sign it, which they subsequently did. But what of the third man, Coleman? Could there be a more sinister reason for the presence of the three white officers alone in the sheriff's office with the young black man on the night he made the statement that helped to condemn him, the defence attorney wanted to know? How voluntary was a confession made in such circumstances? Alexander did his best to press the point home in his cross-examination:

'*Alexander*: Does it take three to take one statement?

Adcock: That was – three was there that day.

Alexander: Well, are three required?

Adcock: No, it could have been four or five there.

Alexander: Especially if only one person was doing the questioning, why were the other two there?

Adcock: We were there to witness the statement.

Alexander: But only two of you witnessed it, isn't that right? Only two of you signed the statement as witnesses.

Adcock: Yes, sir.

Alexander: What was the third one doing there?

Adcock: As a witness, the same as I was there.

Alexander: He was also there as a witness?

Adcock: Right.

Alexander: And you are telling the jury he was not there as added intimidation?

Adcock: That's what I am telling the jury, we wasn't trying to intimidate him.

Alexander: You are telling the jury the third man was not there solely for the purpose of intimidating this defendant?

Adcock:	That's what I'm saying.
Alexander:	OK, and you are telling the jury he was not there solely to supply added manpower and added firepower, if necessary?
Adcock:	I don't understand what you are getting at.
Alexander:	Do you know what manpower is?
Adcock:	This was a voluntary statement he gave. Nobody forced him.
Alexander:	My question is very easily answered, isn't it? The third man was not there to supply added manpower and added firepower.
Adcock:	Was not.
Alexander:	OK. He was there to witness the statement?
Adcock:	I believe I have answered that.
Alexander:	Was your answer yes?
Adcock:	I answered yes.
Alexander:	Even though he did not sign the statement as a witness?
Adcock:	He did not?'

The questioning was laboured, but the young defence attorney made the point in the end. It was not an easy task to get these hard-bitten lawmen to answer a straight question, especially when they were perfectly aware of the traps that Alexander was setting for them. Sheriff Joe Mack Thaggard was an even tougher nut to crack.

Sheriff Thaggard was a lawman of the old school, six foot six tall, an imposing figure from his ten-gallon hat down to his snakeskin cowboy boots, known as 'shit-kickers' because of their pointed, metal-capped toes. He chewed tobacco constantly and had a habit of spitting it at the feet of the person with whom he was speaking, while peering at them through dark, reflecting sun-glasses. It was he who had written the statement down. He had done so, he told the court, word for word as Edward had spoken it. The sheriff was not a literate man. Far from it. He even volunteered the information to the court that Edward had helped him with some of the spelling. There was little call for literary talents in the sheriff's line of work. If Edward's statement bore all the hallmarks of 'police speak', it was not obvious to Joe Mack Thaggard. Many years in the police force seemed to have lulled him into believing that there was nothing abnormal about a young black man talking in such jargon. The sheriff's insistence that the statement was word for word as Edward had spoken it was one of the few gifts the young defence attorney was to receive. Even the sheriff could be

made to look at best a fool, at worst a liar on this issue. All Alexander had
to do was establish the sheriff's position as follows:

'*Alexander:*   Is the statement in your own handwriting?
Sheriff: Yes, sir.
Alexander: Is it your wording?
Sheriff: No, sir.
Alexander: As you read the statement, is it your testimony that every
        word in the statement is a word that was recited to you by
        the defendant?
Sheriff: Yes, sir. I wrote it down as he told it.
Alexander: Word for word?
Sheriff: Yes, sir.'

Then the defence attorney pounced:

'*Alexander:*   So, it is your testimony the defendant talks just like it is in
        that statement?
Sheriff: Yes, sir.
Alexander: All right. Sheriff, would you read the first three sentences
        of the statement, please.'

The sheriff did so.

'*Alexander:*   So, he began, "I, Edward Earl Johnson"?
Sheriff: I started it with his name, yes, sir . . .
Alexander: So, read on after the beginning.
Sheriff: " . . . running south beside the Walnut Grove old bank
        building, or now the drugstore, in my 1972 Buick Electra,
        225, green in colour, I went up to . . ."
Alexander: Excuse me, sheriff, before you read on. Are you testifying
        now that he gave those details in that manner in a
        conversational tone at that time?
Sheriff: Yes, sir.
Alexander: So, that's the way he ordinarily speaks, is that right?
Sheriff: Yes, sir, to my knowledge.
Alexander: To your knowledge, he ordinarily says things like, "I drove
        my 1972 Buick automobile, green in colour"? That's the
        way he ordinarily talks?
Sheriff: Yes, sir.'

It was patent nonsense. But the sheriff had been caught in a trap of his own making. Having insisted that the statement was written down in Edward's own words he had to continue the charade or else show himself up to be a liar and cast doubt on the reliability of his other testimony. Alexander took the sheriff right through the confession, sentence by sentence, forcing the officer to concede that at the very least the statement was not all it appeared to be, that it had been made as the result of interrogation.

'*Alexander:*   So, the statement that was given was not a narrative statement, was it? It was a question and answer conversation, wasn't it?

Sheriff: I wrote down what he told me as to what happened.

Alexander: Did you understand my question, sheriff? The statement as it is written there indicates that he just gave a narrative statement, without any questions being asked, doesn't it? From looking at that statement, it would appear that he just gave a narrative statement, isn't that right?

Sheriff: I don't know whether it would appear that way or not.

Alexander: Well, there are no questions indicated there, are there?

Sheriff: No, sir. There's no questions asked on it.

Alexander: But there were, in fact, questions asked during the statement, were they not?

Sheriff: Yes, sir. I had to ask him questions to be sure as to whether or not I knew what he was talking about.

Alexander: And as a matter of fact, none of your questions are listed?

Sheriff: No, sir.

Alexander: OK. So, as a matter of fact, sheriff, you would ask questions, and he would respond, and then you would word the answers, wouldn't you?

Sheriff: No, sir.'

Alexander then drew the court's attention to the number of times that Edward seemingly referred to himself as 'I, Edward Earl Johnson', six in total.

'*Alexander:*   That was you inserting Edward Earl Johnson?

Sheriff: Yes, sir.

Alexander: Is that correct? Now, sheriff, why was it that you put "I, Edward Earl Johnson" instead of just "I"?

Sheriff:	Put his name down there, so we would know who "I" was and who we were talking about.
Alexander:	Well, it was his statement, wasn't it?
Sheriff:	Yes, sir.
Alexander:	Well, it would be obvious who "I" was, wouldn't it?
Sheriff:	Yes, sir, it could have been.
Alexander:	If he was going to sign it?
Sheriff:	Yes, sir.
Alexander:	But you put that in there yourself?
Sheriff:	Yes, sir.
Alexander:	For a reason, didn't you, sheriff?
Sheriff:	Put his name down, yes, sir.
Alexander:	You wanted to nail it down as far as you could, didn't you?
Sheriff:	I wanted to take the statement down correct and accurate.
Alexander:	You wanted to nail it down and be sure his name appeared as many times on that statement as possible, didn't you?
Sheriff:	No, sir, not necessarily.
Alexander:	And that's why you inserted all the details, like "I drove my 1972 green Buick Electra", and that's why you inserted those details, isn't it, sheriff?'

Next Alexander set out to prove that not only was the statement patently not written in Edward's words, it also contained no information that the police were not already aware of at the time the confession was made.

'*Alexander:*	... Now the information that is contained in that statement, really didn't come as a surprise to you, did it, sheriff?
Sheriff:	What he told me?
Alexander:	Yes.
Sheriff:	I don't recall whether it surprised me or not.
Alexander:	It didn't surprise you? Those facts were things you were familiar with, weren't they?
Sheriff:	I wasn't familiar with the facts that he told me, no sir.
Alexander:	OK. Now, were you – you had talked to Mrs Franklin hadn't you?
Sheriff:	Yes, sir.
Alexander:	And she had told you that someone had attacked her?
Sheriff:	Yes, sir.
Alexander:	And didn't she tell you that the person who attacked her had asked for cologne?

Sheriff:	Yes, sir.
Alexander:	And hadn't she told you the person – that she had inserted the money under the screen?
Sheriff:	She told me he had give her some money, yes, sir.
Alexander:	OK, and that she had inserted the change under the screen?
Sheriff:	She had – yes, sir, she had inserted some change back to him.'

And so on and so forth. Alexander took the sheriff right through the confession arguing that all the detail it contained was already known to the officer at the time it was made. Even the route thought to have been taken by the murderer in his car after the killing had been noted by wakeful Walnut Grove residents and subsequently reported to the police. 'You could have done it [written the statement] without even talking with the defendant, couldn't you?' Alexander queried. The sheriff had no alternative but to admit that he was in possession of most of the facts, although he persisted in claiming that there were pieces of information in the confession that he had not been aware of. No, he did not know that the marshal had been struck on the forehead but, yes, the body had been examined by a doctor and he did know the details of the other injuries. No, he did not know how the marshal fell to the ground, but, yes, he did know the body had been found on the ground by the car. His responses were open to ridicule if not disbelief. In his anxiety to show that the confession was genuine, the sheriff omitted to mention the only point that would have helped to make his case – the fact that Edward seemingly knew where the marshal's gun could be found. It would at some point demand an explanation.

Having cast doubt on the manner in which the written confession was compiled, Alexander then proceeded to show why it was such a vital piece of evidence in the prosecution case and why, therefore, the sheriff might have felt the need to write it himself. Without Edward's alleged admission that he had attacked Miss Sally and then killed Marshal Trest there was no evidence to link the two events. And if there was no link, there was no motive for the murder.

'*Alexander:*	Isn't it a fact, sheriff, that because you did not have any eyewitnesses to this incident [the murder] that you were very anxious to get a statement?
Sheriff:	Yes, we wanted to get a statement, or any evidence we could concerning the case and whoever was involved.

Alexander:	And isn't it also a fact that because you did not have any eyewitnesses to this incident, the only way that you knew of to connect the incident concerning Mrs Franklin and the shooting of Mr Trest, was through a statement?
Sheriff:	Yes, sir, a statement would have helped in the investigation. Sure would.
Alexander:	So, there was in fact a very large gap in the evidence that had accumulated in your investigation, that could only be filled by a statement, isn't that correct sheriff?
Sheriff:	Yes, sir, a statement would sure make the investigation better. Sure would.
Alexander:	No, that's not my question. My question was, wasn't there a gap in your investigation that could only be filled by a statement?
Sheriff:	Yes, sir.
Alexander:	And that's why, from the very beginning, every time you talked with Edward Earl Johnson, or any other suspect in this investigation, you were doing all that you could to get a statement?
Sheriff:	Yes, sir.
Alexander:	Isn't that correct?
Sheriff:	Yes, sir.
Alexander:	And when you talked with the defendant on the highway, between Walnut Grove, Mississippi, and Jackson, Mississippi, a major purpose of being out there was to question him to determine whether or not he would give you a statement?
Sheriff:	He was under investigation. At any time we could get a statement, we was looking for it, yes, sir.
Alexander:	Now, as far as the statement is concerned, if in fact the defendant had given you a voluntary statement, there would have been no reason why he would have refused to write it out himself, isn't that correct?
Sheriff:	Yes, sir, could have been.
Alexander:	And isn't it also a fact, sheriff, that you wrote the statement out, so that you would be able to be certain that you connected up the elements that you had been unable to connect otherwise?'

If the prosecution, when preparing its case, had feared there would be any doubt about the validity of the written confession, there was an obvious and simple way in which they could have attempted to prove otherwise. They could have introduced into the court as evidence the tape recording of the spoken confession the policeman claimed Edward had given them on the road to Jackson. They did not do so. The reason for the absence of this vital piece of evidence can only be supposition.

Edward's attorneys spent several hours in court eliciting the precise story of how the young black man came to make his damning admission in the police car. Much of the argument took place out of the presence of the jury as the defence lawyers attempted to persuade the judge that this and the subsequent written confession were inadmissable evidence having been gained while Edward was illegally detained. The jury was ordered to retire on numerous occasions during the trial while legal submissions were argued.

It was while the jury was out of court that Edward gave his own version of what happened in the car that day. The jurors were never to know what he had to say as the defence attorneys did not put the young man on the witness stand to testify publicly in his own defence. Surprising though it may seem, it is not uncommon in cases such as Edward's for the accused man not to be given a chance to give his side of the story. When a black man is accused of killing a white man in the Deep South, the defending attorneys' great fear is that he will be so intimidated by his situation, he will do more harm than good by being allowed to speak in front of the jury. Edward had all the appearances of an extremely vulnerable witness – young, immature, scared. He spoke in a whisper during his brief testimony before the judge and was repeatedly asked to speak up. At one point after an objection from Alexander during the District Attorney's cross-examination, the judge intervened to prevent intimidation.

'*Alexander:*   Your Honour, I would ask that counsel not be allowed to intimidate the witness.

Judge: I don't think he is intimidating the witness, but back up just a little bit, Max [the DA].'

It is an oft-used lawyer's tactic to stand so close to a frightened witness that they are almost physically bearing down on them. This, coupled with the right tone of voice, can turn the witness into a lump of putty in the attorney's hands. Perhaps Alexander and Brown were right not to put their client on the stand in front of the jury.

The version of the events in the police car which Edward gave and which the twelve men and women who condemned him were never to hear ran as follows:

'They was questioning about a .25 automatic that I had owned. I told them I didn't know anything about it, that I didn't have the gun any more, that it was stolen, and they didn't believe me. They seemed not to believe me. They kept insisting that I did ... As we got on the Interstate I-20 going to Jackson they asked me over and over again, insisting that I knowed about it, and they said that they knew that I had did the crime, and said I was − I was going to have to admit it, wanted me to tell them about it. I told them I didn't know nothing about it. Then I asked about the polygraph. Asked what was it, and they told me it was a lie detector test, see was I telling the truth or not. That's what Officer Adcock told me. Then from there on, I asked Sheriff Thaggard after I take the polygraph, will I go home. So he − he told me that if I didn't tell him something other than I didn't know nothing about it, that I wouldn't be going home. Pulled the car over to the side. They both turned around and looked at me, and they asked me about it again, about what had happened, that they knew that I did it. I told them that I didn't know anything about it, and Officer Adcock started going over things that, I guess, exactly the way he had it, that he knew, that he was telling me. Like, he knew that I went in Sally Franklin's house. I had broken in through the screen window, and I had attacked her, and I ran out the front door, knocking chairs off the porch and things like that, and he kept asking me to agree with him. So I agreed with him because I was threatened. I had been threatened. I was afraid, and after that point he went on to say how Officer Trest was shot. He was telling me that I was running for my car, and the officer pulled around, got out of his, and I shot him down and he had me agree with everything he said. So, I finally agreed with all that he had said. They turned the tape recorder on, read me my rights on it, and then he had me to go over the story again in my own words, and that was it. Turned back around and brought me back to the Grove.'

There is something strangely curious about Edward's courtroom account of the fateful episode in the police car. The young man was on trial for his life. It was very much in his interests to play up any threat or inducements the officers may have made in order to extract a confession from him. It was his word against that of the two policemen, and even if he did not think he would be believed, he had nothing to lose from testifying that the sheriff had perhaps threatened him with a gun, or with physical violence. It would be only natural to have claimed such intimidation in order to save his own skin. But Edward did not make any such allegations. He was threatened, he said, purely by the fact that he, a black man, was alone in the police car with the two white men. He had been raised in Leake County, Mississippi, and knew the sort of treatment a black man can expect from the law.

But in court the young man could only repeat that he was frightened and wanted to go home. His story had an even greater ring of truth to it if only because he did not overstate his case. He was young, innocent and immature for his age, the sort of youngster who shied away from physical violence of any sort. It did not take much to frighten Edward. All he wanted to do was to go home to his grandmother, on whom he was still very emotionally dependent. In his mind that was the main priority, and if he could not go home until he had confessed, that is what he would do. It was a thought process of child-like simplicity. He would, in fact, do anything, if he thought it meant he could then go home. Later in the courtroom – and again in the absence of the jury – he gave a more detailed account of the incident, starting from the point where he was told he would have to take a lie detector test:

'One of the officers asked me would I be willing to take a polygraph. I told him I didn't know what a polygraph was. I asked him again what it was. He told me would I be willing to take it. I told him yeah, I would, if that meant I could go home, and he said yeah. So, I said I will take it, and then I asked could either one – either of my relatives ride with me down there or else could they follow me. They said they couldn't.'

Under cross-examination by the District Attorney, Edward showed yet more clearly what an easy victim the two police officers had picked. Referring to the incident in the car again, the following dialogue took place:

'DA: Neither one of them ever laid a hand on you, did they?
Edward: They didn't have to.
DA: They didn't threaten to lay a hand on you either, did they, Edward Earl?
Edward: It was a threat to me.
DA: What did they say that threatened to lay a hand on you?
Edward: Said if I didn't tell them something, that I wouldn't be going back home.

DA:	And that's a threat to you?
Edward:	That's a threat to me, the way they was looking. Hands on guns, yeah, that's a threat.'

The DA continued his questioning along the same lines, to make it absolutely plain, if it was not already, that Edward had not suffered any physical violence at the hands of the two officers. He did not seem aware that the answers he received only served to show how unlikely it would be that the young man on trial could have attacked anyone, let alone killed them.

'*DA:*	The whole time that you were in that car, did either one of those men ever reach their hand over the back seat where you were sitting?
Edward:	No.
DA:	At all?
Edward:	No, sir.
DA:	Did they ever holler and scream at you?
Edward:	Yes.
DA:	Which one?
Edward:	You might say both of them.
DA:	Well, what did they say?
Edward:	At one point. Hollering and telling me, "Yeah, you did it, you're going to tell us about it too". Things like that . . .
DA:	. . . Did they hit you?
Edward:	No.
DA:	Did they threaten to hit you?
Edward:	No.
DA:	Did they promise you anything?
Edward:	No.
DA:	Did they tell you they was going to promise you anything?
Edward:	No.
DA:	Did they hold out any kind of reward for you at all?
Edward:	No.
DA:	Did they hold out any hopes of leniency for you?
Edward:	No.'

In other words, Edward himself agreed that he had done as the sheriff and the investigator claimed. He had confessed to the murder and the attack on Miss Sally without any overt threats of violence or inducements.

Alexander did make the point during the cross-examination of Adcock that 'it's easier to question somebody in a patrol car on an interstate highway, when one of the officers is driving, with two officers in a car, than it is, say, in the defendant's living room.' But the judge ruled that such a comment was immaterial.

Although Edward's story and that of the two lawmen were remarkably similar, there were differences. Of the two, Edward's seems the more probable. According to Adcock the three men had been on the road to Jackson for about 30 minutes when Edward slid forward on the back seat and said: 'I'm going to tell you about it.' Up until that time, Adcock asked the court to believe, the conversation in the car had centred around 'the weather and gardening. Nothing was said about the case, or the gun, or nothing on the way down – while we was in the car. Just general talk.' He did agree that Edward had asked about the polygraph test and he had told the young man it would not hurt. But apart from that reference, according to the police officers, the three men could have been out for a nice afternoon drive in the country. As Jess Brown queried sardonically: 'Y'all was giving him candy and chewing gum and stuff. He [Edward] just up and said that he wanted to tell you all about it? . . . You didn't stop and buy him pops and hamburgers and all that sort of thing, and let him smoke good cigars? You didn't do that did you?'

The sheriff even maintained in court that Edward had been quite free to leave the car whenever he felt like it.

'*Alexander:*   Officer Thaggard, at the time that the statement was given on the highway, was the defendant free to leave?

Sheriff: Yes, sir.

Alexander: And how could he exercise his freedom on the highway?

Sheriff: Well, he could have gotten out of the car.

Alexander: And walked back to Walnut Grove?

Sheriff: Well, if he – ever how he saw fit to gotten back to Walnut Grove. If he had gotten out of the car, he wouldn't have been wanting to ride with us.

Alexander: . . . Once he stepped into the car on his way to Jackson when you say he was in your custody, you mean he was totally within your control, don't you?

Sheriff: No, sir, I didn't mean he was under my control.

Alexander: Well, the only way he was going to get back to Walnut Grove was to either walk back or hitch a ride, if he decided to leave your company, isn't that right? Isn't that what you just said?

Sheriff:	Yes, sir. If he had elected to get out.
Alexander:	He could have gotten out and walked, is that right?
Sheriff:	Yes, sir.
Alexander:	Of course, if he didn't do that, if he wanted to ride with you, what would he have to do?
Sheriff:	If he had wanted to ride with me, just would have done I assume, what he done.
Alexander:	What is that?
Sheriff:	Rode back with us, or rode on with us to the point where we put him under arrest.'

Did the sheriff have a smile on his face during this exchange, one wonders? If he did, it was probably a little less broad a few minutes later when Alexander returned to the same theme to determine whether Edward had agreed voluntarily to take the lie detector test.

'*Alexander:*	If he [Edward] then refused to continue to Jackson to take the polygraph examination, his alternative was to walk, wasn't it?
Sheriff:	If he refused to take it – not necessarily.
Alexander:	Isn't that what you testified to a few minutes ago?
Sheriff:	I testified if he didn't want to ride in the car, his only alternative would have been to walk.
Alexander:	And the only place you were going was Jackson, wasn't it? So, if he didn't want to ride to Jackson, his only alternative was to walk?
Sheriff:	That's where he had agreed to go, to Jackson, to take the polygraph test.
Alexander:	My question is – the answer to my question is that's correct, that that's where he had to go if he was going to ride with you, because that's where you were going, is that right?
Sheriff:	That's where he had agreed to go with us, yes, sir.
Alexander:	So, if he had changed his mind and didn't want to go to Jackson, and wanted to go somewhere else, he would have to get out and walk, wouldn't he, because you were going to Jackson?
Sheriff:	Well, if he had changed his mind and not wanted to take the polygraph test, our only alternative would have been to turn around and come back.
Alexander:	But that's not what you said a few minutes ago, is it? You

said if he had changed his mind, he could have gotten out
and walked. Isn't that what you testified, sheriff?

Sheriff: I probably misunderstood your question.'

Edward's own feelings about his freedom, or lack of it, were, not
surprisingly, rather different. It was quite simple, 'My understanding was
that I couldn't leave, because they wasn't going to let me,' Edward told his
attorney during questioning in court. Later during cross-examination, the
DA asked him: 'Why didn't you tell them [the police] to turn around and
take you back?' 'I don't think they would have did that,' replied Edward.
'Did you tell them that?' queried the DA. 'I didn't have to,' said Edward.
'Why not?' pursued the DA. 'They wouldn't,' Edward responded. 'How
do you know?' asked the DA. 'I tried not to go in the first place,' replied
Edward.

Much to the eventual impatience of the judge, the prosecution and
defence lawyers spent a total of seven hours going over the circumstances
of Edward's ride in the police car and its results, in an attempt to prove
whether he had or had not been a virtual prisoner at the time. It was a
crucial point for both sides because, if Edward's attorneys had convinced
the judge that their client had been illegally detained and forced to make
a confession under pressure, that confession could not have been
introduced as evidence and read to the jury. There would then have been
no direct link between the murder and the assault. The state would
have been faced with the predicament of making the link between
the attack on Sally Franklin and the murder, a connection they had
to make if her identification of Edward as the killer was to carry any
weight.

But the judge maintained that he was not convinced by what he had
heard from the defence. 'I have now heard considerable testimony from
the very beginning about unlawful detention, suppression, custody and
otherwise,' said Marcus Gordon, 'and in my opinion, there has been no
violation of this defendant's constitutional rights to the point of the
testimony I have now heard. It is the opinion of the court that this
statement should be admitted into evidence and presented to the jury for
their consideration, for their acceptance or rejection ... I am simply
ruling as a matter of law as to the admissability, not to the correctness or
otherwise, but to allow the jury to pass upon that particular item of
evidence.'

But, having lost the battle over the legal submission to prevent
Edward's confession being heard by the jurors, Alexander seemed to

consider it hardly worth fighting the issue any further when the jury returned. Most of the arguments he had put forward in Edward's defence concerning the confession were never re-stated before the jury. After almost a whole day of questioning on the admissability of the evidence, the issue of the confession was over and done with in a relatively short time in the presence of the jury the following day. Edward's attorneys seemed to be losing heart. It was, perhaps, understandable. They had already lost their fight to prevent Sally Franklin pointing the finger at Edward in court.

Seven
Miss Sally

If any one person were to be held responsible for Edward's fate in the Mississippi gas chamber, it would be the 71-year-old lady who gave the jury such a graphic account of her ordeal on the night of the murder of Marshal Jake Trest; the old lady who publicly, in front of the twelve jurors, denounced Edward as the man who had attacked her so violently.

'Is the man that attacked you there in your house that night in this courtroom today?' asked the District Attorney, when Miss Sally took to the witness stand on the second day of the trial. 'Yes, sir,' replied the redoubtable Miss Sally. 'He's sitting right over there,' and she pointed her finger at the young black man sitting next to his two attorneys.

If anyone should know, she should. She had seen her attacker when she went to answer the knock at the door, she had fought with him in her house for several minutes according to her testimony, she even knew who Edward was, had known him since he was a small child. She was positive that Edward was the man, she told the jury. But that was not the whole of the story. If it had been, Brown and Alexander might as well have packed up and left at that point. There was however more to the tale than that, much more, and a great part of that story Miss Sally was not at all happy to reveal to the jury. It would have to be dragged out of her, nugget by nugget.

Sally Franklin went to the witness stand and fought her corner in the best traditions of a heavy-weight boxer, exchanging verbal punch for punch with the defence attorneys as they probed her tale for its weaknesses. In the state of Mississippi where the tough survive, they did not come much tougher than Miss Sally. Old and small she may have been, but frail in spirit or body she most definitely was not. She was a product of the frontier traditions of rural Mississippi womenfolk, who are as capable of wielding a shotgun as their menfolk.

Miss Sally was a well-known character in Leake County. At the time of the trial she had lived in Walnut Grove for the previous 38 years. Through her marriage to the community's doctor, for whom she had worked as a nurse, she had achieved a prominent position in local society. Her husband had died many years before but Miss Sally had continued to live in the large house in the centre of the town adjacent to the doctor's surgery. She took in the occasional lodger and rented out some of her land to poor whites living in trailer homes, but she had no need of any help or assistance. Miss Sally was an independent old woman, well used to looking after herself.

She told the court as much when, during an exchange with Alexander, she described how she had been attacked on the night of the murder. 'He [the attacker] met me in the door and he grabbed this arm, he hit me so hard, if it had been anybody else he would have – he would have killed them right there. He would have knocked them in the head, but my head was so hard, he didn't – he didn't bust my skull. He tried to,' she said. A very tough old lady indeed to be able to fight off a fit, well-built eighteen-year-old youth intent on rape or robbery.

For the prosecution, the problems with Miss Sally's identification evidence were two-fold. Firstly, although she maintained steadfastly in court that Edward was her attacker, her testimony about when she recognised him and to whom she revealed this information was not consistent. She changed her story several times. Secondly her version of events did not tie in with that of other witnesses, including the sheriff.

The first question to cause difficulties was at what point did Miss Sally know that Edward was her attacker? When did she recognise him as the young man who beat her senseless, a man who, she said, she knew well and had seen to speak to just three months prior to the attack? Surely there should be a simple answer. Was it when he came to her door? Was it when he attacked her in the house? Was it when he was brought to her house the following morning to be measured, according to the police, against the height of her door? No, it was on none of these occasions. The police had no firm evidence on which to charge Edward until he confessed to the crime in the police car. Until that point, they had by their own admission, been rounding up any likely suspects in the area, anyone who was young and black. For that, seemingly, was almost all that Miss Sally had been able to tell the police about the man who attacked her.

Almost all, that is. Unfortunately for the investigators of the crime, the only real piece of information provided by Miss Sally was worthless –

even counter-productive in terms of closing the case against Edward. When the police first arrived at Miss Sally's home after the attack, she had in fact been able to put a name to her assailant. But it was not that of Edward Earl Johnson. It was that of another young black man by the name of Fred Smith, who had, according to Miss Sally, announced himself as such when he woke her up to pay his sister's cosmetics bill. The police had gone immediately to the home of Fred Smith and roused his mother and the rest of the family from their beds. But there was a problem. Fred Smith was not there. He could not be. He was in prison serving a sentence for the use of drugs.

By Miss Sally's own testimony in court, she had had a good enough look at her attacker to be able to know it was Edward. But if she was able to see that the man who said he was Fred Smith, was not Fred Smith, why did she maintain it was when the police arrived? Why did she even go along with the cosmetics bill transaction if the man at the door was not the person he claimed to be? If she could see him well enough to know it was Edward, why could she not see that it was not Fred Smith?

Be that as it may, having established that the real Fred Smith had the irrefutable alibi of being in prison, the police were left, they said, with very little to go on in terms of identification. It was not until Sunday evening, after Edward had been arrested and charged with murder and after Miss Sally had seen him going by in a police car, that she suddenly 'remembered' that the man who had attacked her was Edward Johnson. This 71-year-old lady, who the day before had, by her account, suffered a savage beating was actually driving to Jackson pulling a boat she had hooked to the car herself, when it came to her that Edward was the man.

'*Miss Sally:*	When I – when it come to me how he looked and who it was, I was almost to Jackson. I had rented the trailer and they called me to come and close out the deal, and I had to go when the man – the people would be there, and had to move some stuff. So, I got the boat hooked on to the car to move the stuff out of the trailer, and I went on down there, and we tended to that. I rented the trailer and they put the stuff on the boat and started on to Jackson, and I got nearly to Jackson, and it come to me just as plain who it was, how he looked and everything.
Alexander:	What day was this?
Miss Sally:	It was on Sunday, late Sunday evening.'

That is what she told the jury on the second day of Edward's trial. It is not what she said in court at the *habeas* hearing a month after his arrest when she was called to give evidence to establish there was a reasonable case to be answered. On that occasion Jess Brown was her questioner.

'*Miss Sally:*   The sheriff come back to my house Sunday morning.
Brown: Sunday morning?
Miss Sally: And he asked me, said "Are you sure, can you be sure, that's the boy?" and I said. "Yes, that's the boy" . . .
Brown: So, the sheriff came back the following Sunday morning and asked if you were sure?
Miss Sally   Told me, "I want you to be sure. Don't get the wrong one." I told him again, I said "Same height, same colour skin and same voice," and I said, "I'm sure that's who it is." '

In the intervening months between that hearing and the trial, Miss Sally changed her story. She had to. The prosecution had realised by then that evidence of Edward's arrest based on Miss Sally's identification after she had seen him at her home a few hours after the murder and been made aware that he was a suspect, would destroy their case. Placing one lone suspect before a victim and asking if he is the one, is illegal. They have a word for that situation in the United States: it is called a 'show-up' and it is not allowed. For identification evidence to be of any use before an arrest, the suspect must be picked out from an identity parade, or 'line-up'. The sheriff knew that. In his testimony at the trial the following exchange took place:

'*Alexander:*   Is it your testimony today Mrs Franklin never identified this defendant?
Sheriff: She never done a visible identification of him any time. He was never carried before her to be identified visibly.
Alexander: What kind of identification was there, sheriff?
Sheriff: I just testified earlier the only time that I know that she made any type of identification was downtown, some two or three days after the arrest.
Alexander: So, then Mrs Franklin never called you on Sunday and said, "I'm sure he is the one"?
Sheriff: Not that I remember.
Alexander: And she never told you that on Saturday?
Sheriff: No, sir.'

So according to the sheriff, Miss Sally did not name Edward as the attacker until after the investigation was over and Edward was charged. That evidence also conflicted with another part of Miss Sally's testimony because she was quite clear that she had seen Edward at her house on Saturday after he had been picked up for questioning.

'*Alexander:*   That wasn't a line-up they had out at your house on Saturday, was it? They didn't have a number of people there for you to chose between, did they? They just brought one person out there for you to look at?

Miss Sally   I don't know −

Alexander: Is that right, Mrs Franklin?

Miss Sally: − what − I don't know what they had on the outside. I just seen this one person.

Alexander: And that's the only person you saw that day, the only person that was brought there for you to look at?

Miss Sally: As far as I remember, it was.

Alexander: And you couldn't identify that person, even, could you?

Miss Sally: No, I told him I couldn't identify him.

Alexander: So, they had a one-man line-up, and you couldn't pick the defendant out of a one-man line-up?

Miss Sally: You couldn't either if you had been beat half to death.

Alexander: But you were able to do it after you saw him a couple more times, isn't that right?'

Edward's grandmother, Jessie Mae, told the court a similar story. She had followed the police car that had taken Edward to Miss Sally's home and had gone into the house to discover what was happening to him. Since she knew Miss Sally well from the days when she used to work for her, nobody at first showed any surprise at her presence, although later the sheriff told her to leave. Before that happened, however, Edward was brought into the room where both Jessie Mae and Miss Sally sat, and Miss Sally told the sheriff quite definitely that Edward was not the man who attacked her.

These were Jessie Mae's words: 'I was setting side of her [Miss Sally], and she looked up and so she says, "He ain't the one". Said, "This person was low and chunky with a high Afro and chins all on his beard." Well, I knowed he [Edward] didn't have no chin beard. I knowed he didn't have no chin beard because he ain't never growed none . . . She [Miss Sally] said, "He ain't the one".' Jessie Mae's evidence about the assailant being 'low and chunky' was not repeated by any of the prosecution witnesses.

Edward was tall and of medium build. He did not fit that description at all.

Miss Sally had an explanation for all the inconsistencies and contradictions in her account of what had happened. She was suffering from shock, she said. 'If you had your brains about half beat out, you might not think of it in three or four days, and it might be two or three months,' she told Alexander. That would seem quite a reasonable explanation if the court had been dealing with the average 71-year-old lady who had been nearly murdered in her own home. It is even conceivable that Miss Sally, tough as she was, may have suffered some ill effects after such a violent attack. But by her own account, she did not. The following day she was on the telephone making some sort of business deal, hitching a boat up to her car and driving about 50 miles to the state capital of Jackson to go fishing on the nearby Ross Barnett reservoir.

It was a remarkable recovery. Perhaps she had been less severely beaten than she maintained. Some of the evidence given by the doctor who examined her after the attack would give support to the theory that Miss Sally had exaggerated her description of the attack. At the pre-trial hearing four weeks after Edward's arrest, Dr David Moody told the court that he had examined Miss Sally immediately afterwards and again the following day, had found no fractures or serious injuries, nor had he prescribed any medication for her. She had not required any treatment at all.

But at the trial he gave a detailed account of the bruises and abrasions he had found on Miss Sally's body and confirmed that she was in a state of shock. He had prescribed analgesia, he told Alexander. But when pressed by the young attorney it became apparent that the 'prescription' was nothing more than aspirin. 'She had aspirin already there,' Dr Moody conceded. 'She asked if it was OK and I told her to go ahead and take some aspirin if she felt like she needed it.'

Miss Sally's identification of Edward as her assailant was obviously much weaker than it appeared when she pointed him out to the jury in the courtroom. Most prosecution witnesses will point out the defendant if asked to do so in court. But as with the confession evidence, Alexander's legal submission to have Miss Sally's identification testimony ruled inadmissable were doomed to failure. His arguments were not accepted by the judge. In his ruling on the issue Marcus Gordon said: 'From the great conflict in the testimony, I cannot rule that this motion [Alexander's arguments] to suppress the identification should be sustained. I would expect that these issues would be presented to the jury as a question of fact for the jury to decide.'

Whatever the judge and jury may have thought, it would appear, if the confusing testimony is to be believed, that Miss Sally did not know who her attacker was until after Edward was arrested. In which case, why did the sheriff select the young man, one out of many who were fingerprinted and interrogated on Saturday, as his prime suspect and the one who was asked to take the lie detector test in Jackson? There were three reasons, the sheriff told the court. Edward drove a car similar to one that had been seen in the area after the murder; he had scratches on his hands and legs, which might have indicated that he had been in a fight; and he owned a gun similar to the .25 automatic found at the scene of the murder. Taken individually the evidence given in court on all three so-called suspicious circumstances amounted to very little indeed.

Number one was the car. Edward owned an old Buick, a fact the police were aware of when they first picked him up as he was doing some repair work on it at the time. The car had two distinguishing features. It had a CB antenna and this particular model had tail lights running almost continuously across the back. A witness was produced in court by the District Attorney who stated that he had seen a car with similar tail lights and antenna stopped outside his house on the outskirts of Walnut Grove shortly after Jake Trest was murdered. Morris Tucker told the jury he had been roused from his sleep by a telephone call from his son-in-law to tell him there was trouble in Walnut Grove, had looked out of his window and seen the car, which appeared to have stalled. It was, in the words of Edward's statement, green in colour. He had reported what he saw to the sheriff the next morning. A second witness, a neighbour of Miss Sally's by the name of Robert Wright, testified he had seen a car with similar tail lights driving down the road shortly after he had been woken by the sound of shots. No proof was put forward to show that these two sightings were of the same car or that it could be linked to the murder. In addition one of the deputy sheriffs who first picked Edward up, admitted under questioning from Jess Brown that the features described on the vehicle were not particularly unusual in the area.

There was no dispute about the fact that Edward had scratches on his legs and hands. He told the sheriff he had received them in a fight with another man at the chicken-processing factory where he worked. In view of the fact that Edward was said by those who knew him well to have avoided violent confrontations, it was perhaps surprising that he should have been involved in a fight. But his story was backed up by two witnesses. Edward's aunt, Thelma, told the court she had seen the scratches on the young man when he returned from work on the day before the murder, and, more importantly, another young man called Wilson Smith testified that he had indeed had a fight with Edward at work and that he had told the police about it on Saturday when they questioned him as part of their investigation.

Perhaps the testimony about the murder weapons would provide the jury with more conclusive evidence of guilt. Edward admitted that he used a gun. It would have been unusual if he had not. It is a common sight in Leake County to see pick-up trucks driving around with several rifles stacked in the back. Many people also keep a hand gun in their vehicles. On the outskirts of nearly every small community there are shacks masquerading as pawn shops with garish signs offering to loan money on guns, gold, silver. When first questioned about the murder, Edward said he used his grandmother's gun. Jessie Mae was asked to produce it, and did so. He later said he had had a .25 automatic of his own but this had been stolen from his car. Another young black man called Eli Boler, who also worked with Edward, was called to the witness stand by the prosecution to testify that about two weeks before the murder he had seen a .25 automatic in the glove compartment of Edward's car.

This was the only evidence that the District Attorney introduced to link Edward with either of the murder weapons. Two guns were produced in court as evidence, a .25 automatic and a .357 Smith & Wesson. The .25 was linked directly to the shooting by a ballistics expert who said the bullets found in Jake Trest's body matched those from the weapon. There was no such evidence to link the powerful .357 to the shooting. No fingerprint evidence was given for either weapon despite the fact that a print expert had been called to the scene of the crime and both guns had, according to other evidence, been retrieved without disturbing possible fingerprints. Were there no fingerprints or did they not match those of the man in the dock?

The .25 had been found at the scene of the crime, having slipped from the murderer's hand when he used it to strike the marshal on the head, the prosecution maintained. In that case there had obviously been no opportunity to wipe it clean. The .357 had been discovered on some scrubland outside Walnut Grove the day after Edward was charged. The police search had been directed to that area, the prosecution case claimed, because in his confession Edward had said that he had thrown the gun from his car and pinpointed the precise location. If that was so, he could have wiped it clean. But there was no evidence that this was the case, nor was there any scientific evidence that the weapon produced in court was the one that fired fatal bullets. Why not? The jury was never to know. Alexander and Brown failed to raise any of these questions in cross-examination.

The District Attorney must have been agreeably surprised that the evidence he put forward concerning the murder weapons was virtually unchallenged. He obviously thought that the case against Edward needed some extra backing for on the final day of the prosecution evidence he produced two surprise witnesses to put the final nail in the coffin. He had been allowed to introduce his evidence of confession, he had been allowed to introduce his evidence of identification, but, just in case there should be anyone on the jury left in any doubt, he produced, like rabbits out of a hat, two people who would swear that Edward had personally admitted his guilt to them.

If anyone in the courtroom in Carthage during the preceding four days was beginning to wonder if this trial was not making a mockery of justice, these two star prosecution witnesses would have put the seal on it. Who were they? One was seventeen-year-old Steve Brown, the son of Deputy Sheriff Bobby Brown, the man who had accompanied Sheriff Joe Mack Thaggard to the murder scene and who combined his deputy sheriff duties with those of Carthage jailer. The other was Sammy Jamison, a prisoner in that jail, who had been in and out of the prison on so many occasions over recent years that he had been made a trusty because, in his own words, 'they got tired of turning the key'. The DA could not have produced less credible witnesses if he had tried. Both of these witnesses said they had talked to Edward while he had been held in the jail awaiting trial. When the jailer's son was asked by the DA if he had discussed the murder with Edward, the boy gave the following reply: 'I asked him [Edward], 'How come you to do something like that?' He said, 'Well, I wasn't sorry about doing it.' Fellow prisoner Sammy Jamison was asked a similar question. 'He [Edward] just said that he ran up on the guy at Walnut Grove, and they got in an argument, and he shot him, and that was all,' said the trusty.

Even an inexperienced defence lawyer could have driven a horse and cart through evidence from such obviously biassed witnesses. But for Edward, Brown and Alexander, the three black men seated at the table in front of the judge and jury, it had almost ceased to matter by then. The trial was all but over. Given the judge's strict schedule it had only two more days to run at the most, and the defence had not even started to put forward their case. There was the final summing up from both sides to come as well. And who knew how long the jury would take to reach a verdict? What did it matter if the DA produced plausible or implausible witnesses to say that Edward had killed Marshal Trest? He could probably have got the whole of the white community in Leake County to stand up and say that Edward had confessed to the murder. In such circumstances it must have seemed to Brown and Alexander that trying to discredit the two surprise witnesses was so much wasted breath.

Eight

The Verdict is Death

The defence attorneys need not have feared that there would not be enough time for the jury to give proper consideration to its verdict. It took those twelve men and women a mere 29 minutes to pronounce Edward guilty — 29 minutes from the time they left their seats in the courtroom to the time they returned. It was a unanimous decision. Edward was guilty of capital murder.

The jurors had heard almost five days of conflicting evidence upon which a man's life depended. They had been instructed by the judge to retire to the jury room and consider that evidence. They had been told they must select a foreman or forelady. They had been further ordered to read and digest several pages of complicated instructions concerning the law and capital murder, instructions which the judge together with the four attorneys had agreed after lengthy discussion in chambers. They must decide not only whether Edward was guilty or not, but whether the crime was capital murder, which carries the death penalty, or simple murder, which does not. They succeeded in accomplishing all that in less than half an hour. It did not allow much time for serious deliberation — hardly enough for the foreman to ask each juror for his answer to the question: 'Guilty or not guilty?'

Admittedly in the latter stages of the trial the defence attorneys had not provided much new evidence for them to consider. They had produced three character witnesses who testified to Edward's good reputation and two or three relatives and friends to back up some of the points already brought out in the cross-examination of prosecution witnesses. In addition four people had been put on the witness stand to provide Edward with an alibi. They testified that they had been with the young man at a card game the night of the murder until about 2.00 in the morning. Since, during the trial the prosecution witnesses had all sworn to the fact that the attack on Miss Sally and subsequent murder took place after 2.30 am, the alibi as heard by the jury was useless. It allowed Edward plenty of time to drive from the house where he was playing cards to Miss Sally's home. It was a gross piece of incompetence by Alexander and Brown for, many years later, when Clive Stafford Smith went to Walnut Grove to investigate the crime, he found numerous people who would have testified to seeing Edward much later than 2.00 am, thus providing him with a semblance of a watertight alibi.

The case for the defence lasted less than three hours. The summing up process was equally brief, for Marcus Gordon limited the speech of each lawyer to no more than an hour – and appointed someone to keep an eye on a stop-watch in case anyone was tempted to overrun his allotted time. Jess Brown, who led off for the defence, was quick to point out to the jury the speed with which the whole trial had been conducted. Courts will spend weeks trying a simple burglary or assault, he said. Here the jury was faced with evidence about both these crimes in addition to the major one of murder. But his arguments on Edward's behalf were weak and muddled. His speech was garbled. He spent much of his hour trying to suggest that Jake Trest might not have been on duty at the time he was killed, a fact, which if true, could have reduced the charge from capital to simple murder. But Brown's arguments were foolish. 'He [Trest] could have been out there somewhere going to buy some cigars or something. Going around the corner to get some candy or something. Anything,' said Brown. The District Attorney was quick to pick up on this when it came to his turn to speak. 'You don't go get cigars and candy at 2.30 in the morning in Walnut Grove, Mississippi. I know that, and you know it too. He [Brown] ought to know it,' he told the jury. About the only thing which could not be disputed was that Marshal Trest was on duty at the time he was shot and to waste precious time trying to prove otherwise was folly.

Alexander, on the other hand, raised questions that demanded a real explanation.

'The issue is has the state of Mississippi proven to you beyond a reasonable doubt that the defendant was responsible, and no fair-thinking person, no rational or reasonably minded person, could believe that this evidence was sufficient. No-one could. There are absolutely too many gaps in the evidence.

'The first thing is that Mrs Franklin's testimony, assuming that she means as well as she can, just is not reliable. She testified to one thing one day. She testified to one thing yesterday, and she testified to something else again today. She testified to something else even different in Forest last year.

'Sheriff Thaggard got on the stand this morning and testified for fifteen minutes and had his testimony stricken because he did not know what he was talking about. Is that the kind of evidence that you can rely upon to send somebody to jail for the rest of their life or to have them killed?

'That kind of evidence is not sufficient to convict anybody of any crime whatsoever, and here the state of Mississippi comes in here with that kind of evidence, and asks you to convict a person of one of the most serious crimes ever thought of. When you try to charge somebody with capital murder, you ought to have your act together, and this has got to be one of the sloppiest cases I have ever seen presented to any jury with any kind of expectation of a conviction.

'The very idea that they would bring this case before you is an insult to your intelligence,' Alexander went on. Where are the fingerprints on the two weapons? What evidence is there that the Smith & Wesson gun was the one belonging to Jake Trest? Why did the defendant not write his own statement, if it was voluntary? Where is the tape recording? Why was Edward's grandmother not allowed to accompany him in the car? And, crucial to the whole story, 'is this whole case a figment of somebody's imagination as far as what happened at Sally Franklin's house? Is this just something that was conjured up to try to connect and try to give a reason for something that nobody knows why it happened?' The prosecution 'came in here purely and simply with a railroad,' announced the young attorney at the end of an impassioned speech. 'So, you are the only twelve people now to stand between the defendant and a gross miscarriage of justice.'

It took them 29 minutes to decide otherwise. They retired to the jury room with the final words of the District Attorney's speech ringing in their ears. 'It's time, ladies and gentlemen, for us to establish strong law and order in Leake County, Mississippi,' he told them.

'If we are going to live in a civilised society, if we are going to live and raise our families in Leake County, Mississippi, you are not going to be able to let somebody like that, that will do this kind of heinous crime, walk the streets of Leake County . . .

'Ladies and gentlemen, there comes a time when it is time to bite the bullet, and I'm not talking about the way J T Trest did it. I'm talking about get down in that ditch and come into this jury room, get in that jury box, and listen to the witnesses from that stand, take that evidence, and unbiasedly, without any kind of prejudice in your heart, your soul, your mind, analyse that evidence, put aside your connections, put aside how you feel about any kind of prejudice. Look straight from what came from that witness stand and determine that the state of Mississippi has met the burden of proof, and we never shirked it for a minute. We have met the burden of proof beyond a reasonable doubt, and, I submit, to all doubt . . .'

The jury found Edward guilty of capital murder. This eighteen-year-old black youth was most decidedly the violent criminal who had shattered Jake Trest's skull that night in Walnut Grove. But the courtroom ordeal was not yet over for Edward. Having found him guilty, the jury must now decide whether he should live or die. Under American law, the jury is charged with two responsibilities in a capital murder case. It must decide on whether he is guilty or innocent. And then, after the lawyers have had an opportunity to plead for his life, or demand that the ultimate penalty should be paid, it must decide on the sentence to be imposed – imprisonment or death.

Edward was destined to spend a night in his cell waiting to know what the outcome would be. After the verdict was announced, Marcus Gordon adjourned the court until the following day, a Saturday, for the final drama to be played out. This time the judge allowed the attorneys 45 minutes each to make their final speeches. He would have limited them to 30 minutes had not Jess Brown put forward strenuous objections. 'We are arguing . . . whether the man should die or live,' he said. 'We are not dealing with a matter of whether the man should lose his automobile or not, but his life.' Even so Brown was cut off during the course of his closing speech because he overran his 45 minutes.

The time for dealing with the evidence was over. Now was the time for more profound thought. These final speeches provided an opportunity for the lawyers to direct the minds of the jury to the whole issue of execution – the lawful taking of a man's life by the state. Both Brown and Alexander drew on Christian teaching in their efforts to save the life of their client. 'We are talking about the power of life and death,' said Alexander, 'and I don't know what you have been taught, but I always understood that life shouldn't be taken, except by someone who can give life, and I only know of one entity in this universe who can give life. I have never met a man who could give life and I have never known a jury that could give life. That power resides only in God.' What the state of Mississippi is demanding, he said, is not punishment but revenge, retribution.

Brown had a similar message to give. 'If you are Christians, you believe in the Ten Commandments, and one of those Commandments is I shall not kill. There can't be some little man over there in the Legislature write a law and come in here and tell you you can kill this man. Can't do . . . Right now you are God . . . Every one of you are Gods . . . You are his [Edward's] God. That's the thing . . . You can spare his life, or you can kill him.'

The District Attorney rode rough-shod over the ethics of sentencing a man to die. 'You are being fooled,' he said referring to the defence attorney's words. 'You are being carried for them to make you think that the state of Mississippi is asking you to do something wrong. We are not. I'm not playing on your conscience, putting doubts in your mind with statements about Supreme Beings that you won't hear come from my mouth . . . The only thing I'm asking you to do is what the law authorises. I'm not asking for revenge or retribution, or any of the things that people have been up here hollering and screaming at you about. I'm asking for justice.' The murder of Jake Trest was an especially heinous, atrocious and cruel act and for this reason alone, if no other, Edward should be sentenced to die, the DA said. 'How can anybody come to this jury and say look out . . . try to mislead you down the road of thinking that you are fixing to do something wrong when he [Edward] is not sorry for what he has done? Why should you? Why should you go and get out of the ditch and say I care, but he doesn't?'

The jury took one hour and seven minutes to decide on the sentence that Edward must pay for his crime. But, because it failed to record its decision in the proper manner, it was to be a further 26 minutes before the news was announced to those anxiously waiting in the courtroom. 'We unanimously find that the defendant, Edward Earl Johnson, should suffer death,' the circuit court clerk read from the paper on which the sentence had been recorded.

The judge ordered Edward to stand. '. . . In accordance with the verdict of the jury, it is the duty of this Court to pronounce sentence upon you, and I do hereby sentence you to suffer death in the gas chamber of the Mississippi State Penitentiary on the 14th day of October, 1980,' Marcus Gordon proclaimed.

And this burlesque of a trial was not to end there. Against all expectations, there was one final scene yet to be played. The court clerk was not the only one to have trouble with his reading, it appeared. For, while the jury was struggling to record its sentencing decision in the proper manner, Alexander and Brown had asked the judge to order a mis-trial. The reason, they said, was because it had just been brought to their attention that one of the jurors could neither read nor write. It was a grave allegation. Before the trial had begun all the jurors had been asked if they were able to read and write. During their deliberations on Edward's fate, they had been required to read a number of documents informing them of their legal responsibilities as jurors. If it then turned out that a member of that jury was totally illiterate, the judge would have no alternative but to order a new trial. But Marcus Gordon was suspicious. Were the two attorneys trying to manipulate the court, he wondered? It seemed very convenient that Alexander and Brown had only just discovered that the juror could not read or write. If they had notified the court of this fact before the jury retired to consider its verdict, a substitute juror could have been called to serve. One had been present throughout the trial in case a member of the jury had to be released because of illness or some other reason. But that person could not now be called once the verdict had been delivered.

'When did this matter come to your attention,' the judge wanted to know? Both Brown and Alexander assured him they had only learned of it when the jury had retired to consider the sentence. In that case, said the judge, he would hear whatever evidence the defence attorneys had to prove their point. The juror, a 60-year-old black woman, Mrs Eddie Leflore, was called to the witness stand and asked by Alexander to read aloud one of the legal instructions given to the jury. It should have been a simple enough matter to establish whether she could read or not. but it was not to be so. Mrs Leflore proved to be no ally of the defence attorneys. She responded as follows to Alexander's request: 'I'm just going to be honest with you. My eyes is bad, and my blood is so high. See where I got my glasses? I can't hardly hold my eyes open, but now you can ask them in yonder didn't I write my own.'

After further questioning from the judge, it was established that Mrs Leflore had high blood pressure, had not taken her medicine since Monday and was feeling ill and dizzy. At this particular moment she could not read, she said, but she swore that she was normally able to do so. Marcus Gordon was in a quandary. It was by now late on Saturday afternoon. He was due to open a new court in another county on Monday. He felt obliged to let Mrs Leflore go home until she felt better. It appeared that he might have to reconvene the Leake County court at a later date to establish the facts about Mrs Leflore. In the meantime he was uncertain whether the judgement that had been delivered against Edward was valid. It was a legal situation he had not previously encountered. He decided to continue with further evidence on the issue without Mrs Leflore present.

Alexander next called the woman's step-daughter, Mrs Zella Griffin, as a witness. She stated categorically that Mrs Leflore could not read or write. But she also revealed that she had told Edward's aunt, Thelma Johnson, about Mrs Leflore's disability as long ago as Wednesday and that that information had been passed on to other members of the family. These facts were manna from heaven for the District Attorney. If he could prove that Brown and Alexander had known about Mrs Leflore for some time but had concealed their knowledge, the boot would be on the other foot. The legal conundrum could be turned against the defence. The DA decided to investigate further and call his own witnesses. He and his assistant had already made some rapid inquiries among members of Edward's family, and thought they could prove the defence attorneys had withheld the information about Mrs Leflore until it was too late for the court to redress the situation. They were going for the kill a second time, this time against their legal adversaries. The first witness they called was none other than Jess Brown.

Brown was not a good witness. His answers to the DA's questions were vague and strayed from the point. In essence he declared that he had been told about Mrs Leflore at lunchtime that day, but on the other hand he might have been told earlier and forgotten. The two attorneys, the DA and Brown, argued the matter back and forth with a lack of legal discipline more in keeping with a bar-room brawl. Eventually Marcus Gordon decided he could stand no more. He issued a stern warning: 'Now, if I have to put my foot down to whip you fellows in line, I have been on the edge of it several times this week, now I will flat lower the boom on each and every one of you, regardless of which position, you [Brown], your associate, or the prosecuting attorneys, what position you have. Now, we will get back to a little courtroom decorum. All of you.'

Edward's great uncle Irving Parker was then called as a witness by the DA. He admitted having told Brown about Mrs Leflore but said he could not now remember whether he had done that today or the day before, despite the fact that when the assistant prosecuting attorney, Dannye Hunter, had asked him about it outside the courtroom he had said it was the day before. Hunter was also called as a witness and swore that Parker had indeed said that Brown had been told about Mrs Leflore the previous day. The situation was becoming more and more farcical with attorneys from both sides striding backwards and forwards from the witness stand to their lawyers' tables giving evidence in a case on which they were employed and questioning each other about the facts. It seemed highly probable that someone was committing perjury.

At 5.30 on Saturday evening, August 16th, Marcus Gordon decided to call a halt to it. He ruled that the court would reconvene on Monday, September 8th, and in the meantime the defence could go ahead and request a new trial. The two issues to be considered when the court met again were whether Mrs Leflore could read or write, and at precisely what time Jess Brown was made aware of this information.

Mrs Leflore turned up at the special court session as requested but asked to be allowed to go home as she was still ill. She produced a doctor's certificate to this effect, but Marcus Gordon decided she must stay. The matter had to be resolved one way or another. Mrs Leflore took the stand:

'*Alexander:*   Mrs Leflore, I want to hand you state's instruction number S-12 and ask if you would read that instruction to the court.

Mrs Leflore: I really can't, because my eyes are bad. I can write some. Give me a pencil, and I can write. I'm just sick.

Alexander: Mrs Leflore, let me ask you this question again. Are you able to read this instruction?

Mrs Leflore: I told you I wasn't.'

But on further questioning Mrs Leflore claimed that it was her illness that prevented her from reading, not her ability to do so and that she had been able to read during the trial. Alexander pointed out that whatever the problem was, Mrs Leflore had been unable to read the document aloud in court less than an hour after she supposedly read it in the jury room. He then asked her to tell him what she had read in the jury room.

'*Alexander:*   When you said you read these [the documents] in there, what did you read?

Mrs Leflore: I disremember what I read.

Alexander: Do you remember reading anything about aggravating circumstances?

Mrs Leflore: I don't know.

Alexander: Do you remember reading anything about mitigating circumstances?

Mrs Leflore: I don't know.

Alexander: Do you know what aggravating circumstances are?

Mrs Leflore: No, I don't reckon I do.

Alexander:	Do you know what mitigating circumstances are?
Mrs Leflore:	I don't reckon I do. Not now...
Alexander:	Do you remember returning a verdict in this case?
Mrs Leflore:	I don't know. I reckon so.
Alexander:	You don't know?
Mrs Leflore:	Yeah. Yeah, I remember.
Alexander:	Do you remember?
Mrs Leflore:	Yes.
Alexander:	Do you know what the verdict was?
Mrs Leflore:	Sure, I think I do.
Alexander:	What was the verdict?
Mrs Leflore:	I'm just sick now. I don't know. I am just sick.
Alexander:	Now, Mrs Leflore, at this time you do not remember what verdict you rendered in this case? Is that right?
Mrs Leflore:	I reckon I can remember some if I studies it awhile.'

The juror stuck to her story throughout lengthy questioning by both Alexander and the District Attorney. When she was dismissed from the witness stand, no further witnesses were called as the judge had decreed at the start of the morning's proceedings that he would hear only Mrs Leflore. Marcus Gordon had had enough. He was ready to deliver his opinion on the matter: 'Does an education teach a person the difference between right and wrong? Surely, a person who is illiterate, and it is my belief that a person will be able to distinguish between right and wrong. I am never one of those who believes that a degree of education established intelligence, but in all probability, exemplified the opportunity in life, and a great number of people have never had the opportunity in life to go to school and have an education.'

Therefore, he ruled, he would not allow the defence attorneys' request for a new trial based on the fact that Mrs Leflore was illiterate. He also stated on the official record that it appeared to him that Brown and Alexander may well have known of the juror's inability to read and write before the final sentence was announced and had deliberately refrained from making this knowledge public until it was too late to rectify the situation. His statement had serious implications for the two lawyers. At one point it looked as though the trial of Edward Johnson would end with his senior defence attorney being prosecuted himself. Jess Brown said of the whole shambolic incident later: 'the trial itself was a difficult experience. There was an issue concerning a juror, Mrs Leflore, who we heard could not read or write. We held a hearing on that and the District

Attorney put me on the stand as a witness for the prosecution. Then at the end of the hearing, he subpoenaed defence witnesses, as well as Mr Alexander, to appear before the Grand Jury for some charge apparently against me. In the end nothing came of it, but it was very intimidating to me, and made my job representing Mr Johnson more difficult.'

Thus it was that Edward's fate was judicially sealed on September 8th, 1980. Later, many years later, after Clive Stafford Smith was called upon to save the black man in the final weeks of his life, other, even more disturbing evidence was unearthed concerning the impartiality and competence of the jurors, including Mrs Leflore; evidence that would explain the black woman's insistence in the face of all that was reasonable and obvious that she could read. But by then it was too late.

*   *   *

It was not long before the humdrum routine of normal small town Mississippi life returned to the community of Carthage again. People continued to talk about the murder and conviction of Edward Johnson, but the high drama was over for them. Most of the white population of the area were quite happy to forget all about it. They had done their jobs, the murderer had been sentenced, there was no call to lose any sleep over the fate of a hitherto unknown black man. The black community did not forget so easily, nor did they want to, but they kept their peace. There was nothing to be gained from keeping the event alive. Better to let the open hostility aroused return to slumber. It was safer for everyone that way.

But for Edward, by now just turned nineteen, the end of the trial marked the beginning of the final phase of his life. Shortly after the verdict was reached he was transported to the Mississippi State Penitentiary at Parchman, where he was to live like an animal in a cage until his death. For the next seven years he was to know nothing else except the narrow confines of his barred cell on the Mississippi Death Row, and the small exercise yard adjacent to the block where the prisoners are occasionally allowed to feel the air on their faces.

Parchman Penitentiary is the ultimate destination of thousands of Mississippi convicts. Situated in the north-west corner of the state, about 20 miles from the banks of the Mississippi River and 150 miles from Jackson, it was intended to house all the state's long-term prisoners. The prison itself is a collection of low, barrack-like buildings standing within hundreds of acres of flat, featureless farmland. The inmates, apart from those on Death Row, spend their days working in the fields in gangs reminiscent of the slave-owning days of the previous century. They till the soil with hoes and rakes. When it was first built, the surrounding area was owned by local farmers, and the prison was a useful source of free labour. In recent years the penitentiary authorities have farmed the land themselves as a commercial enterprise.

The area in which Parchman lies is known in Mississippi as the Delta, a seemingly inappropriate name for a region several hundreds of miles from the mouth of the great river. But there is a curious geographical rationale to the name. The Mississippi is an unpredictable river. Until fairly recently, when its powerful waters were brought under a semblance of control by man-made means such as high banks known as levees, the river wandered where it willed, looping and turning upon itself so dramatically over the years that many small Mississippi towns, which once earned their livelihood from waterborne trade, are now no longer anywhere near its banks. Frequently it spilled out, drowning huge areas of adjacent countryside. This regular flooding has turned the Delta into a huge, flat, desolate yet fertile expanse. The accumulated silt has made it rich farming land, which springs into life during the summer. In the winter it returns to its natural state, dreary miles of dark brown mud. It is a depressing, sparsely populated landscape. And it is this factor which make the area an ideal site for a prison such as Parchman Penitentiary. The Delta mud offers no refuge or hiding place to an escaped prisoner. Inmates who do seek freedom are usually caught fairly rapidly before they can reach the anonymity and safety of a large city. The tracker dogs see to that.

Parchman Death Row is a prison within a prison. The single storey blocks which house about 40 men are sited away from the main complex. Known officially as the Maximum Security Unit, it resembles a small concentration camp. The buildings are ringed by a fifteen foot wire perimeter fence topped with barbed wire, with watch towers at each corner. Access is gained only through a pair of massive barred gates, operated electronically from the watch tower. A visitor entering the unit is given a taste of captivity. The first gate opens to allow entry and then clangs shut behind, leaving him trapped in a no-man's land. Only then does the second gate open, allowing release into Death Row.

There seems little chance of escape from the place. But the guards take no chances. Edward, like his fellow prisoners, became used to being manacled during the brief periods he was allowed out of his cell or the exercise yard. Movement of any kind is restricted to a slow shuffle, through the use of leg irons, waist chains and handcuffs. In such circumstances, some condemned men come to see death as an escape. And death is ever present. The gas chamber itself is a part of the small complex, clearly visible to the men in the exercise yard. When an execution takes place, or the chamber is being tested to ensure it is in proper working order, the bitter almond smell of the cyanide gas filters through to the prisoners in their adjoining cells.

For Edward those seven years were a long drawn-out death. Precisely how he coped without cracking up under the strain will never be known. There is very little a Death Row prisoner can do to lift the load of impending execution from his mind. Many spend hours each day lying on their bunks watching television. Others make use of the prison library. Like many of his fellow prisoners, Edward developed a heightened appreciation of the smallest contacts with the outside world; the occasional visits from relatives, friends and lawyers; letters or a rare telephone call. So deprived was he of all normal senses and human contact that, shortly before he died, when he was allowed a few extra privileges, he was able to draw comfort from the sight of the moon and the stars which he had not seen for so many years. The men also drew strength from each other. Edward developed a particularly close relationship with another black man, his namesake, Sam Johnson.

Sam is an older man, who was already well into his thirties when he arrived at Parchman shortly after Edward. Now 46, he still waits on Death Row, hoping and praying that he will not suffer the same fate as Edward. Sam too is condemned to die, a convicted murderer who claims he is innocent. But he is a mature man with great intellectual and emotional reserves on which to draw, and the generous nature to share them with others. From his wider experience of the world and adult life, he was able to provide Edward, still scarcely more than a boy, with some of the mental and emotional support that he needed to see him through the years. The two liked to use the exercise yard together, if possible, and often played chess together to provide themselves with mental as well as physical agility. They also met during the weekly visit to the prison law library – a visit which provides Death Row inmates with their constitutional right to research their own cases and compile petitions objecting to prison conditions. For many condemned men it is also an opportunity to get to know each other, exchange gossip and experience something approaching normal human intercourse. Sam and Edward shared many hours together on these visits, much of the time spent waiting in prison vans while the guards dallied over laborious security procedures. They were very close, and when Edward died, Sam grieved as he would for a blood brother.

The monotony of a prisoner's life on Death Row is punctuated by the advances and setbacks he experiences as his case slowly winds its way through the maze of the American legal appeal system. Most condemned men and women in the United States can expect to survive for at least seven years or so after sentence is pronounced, such is the variety of paths their appeals can take. It can and does take years for an appeal to wend its way from the humble state and district courts, to the middle-ranking federal courts, back to the state supreme courts and then, perhaps, finally, up to the US Supreme Court. The prisoner must learn to live with hope and despair as his appeals are agreed, or, more usually, rejected by the individual courts. He must learn to cope with the fact that dates for his execution may be set and deferred at any time during this process. He must keep a hold of his sanity when he comes within weeks, days or even hours of his death before the execution date is stayed, only to be rescheduled for another time. He must learn to live with death.

Edward was no exception to this pattern. Following the trial his lawyers immediately appealed to the Mississippi Supreme Court for a re-hearing of the case. This was denied in June, 1982, and execution was set for the following month. Subsequent requests for the sentence to be overturned were rejected in 1984, 1985 and 1986. Jess Brown continued to represent Edward through all these legal manoeuvres, assisted by a number of different lawyers including at one time James Robertson, who now sits as a judge on the Mississippi Supreme Court.

It was not, however, until April 1987, that Clive Stafford Smith took up the cudgels on behalf of Edward Johnson. At that point Edward had only a month to live. Clive had known Edward for several years, having met him on his frequent visits to Mississippi Death Row to confer with his clients. He knew him as a quiet, gentle person. But he was not familiar with his case as he was only called upon to represent him when it appeared to other lawyers that all hope was lost and all legal avenues had been explored unsuccessfully. Clive is renowned for his legal expertise and dedication. If anyone could save Edward now, those who cared for him thought, it would be the young Englishman. On 24th April, with the execution date set for 20th May, Clive was asked to take on the case. He had little time within which to operate. Because of prior commitments to other Death Row clients, he was not even able to start work on the case until 3rd May, only seventeen days before the scheduled execution.

Clive's first task was to bring himself up to date on the case and read the trial transcript of about 3,000 pages. He spent many hours with Edward in his prison cell, talking not only about the events leading up to his arrest, but also about his early life, his family, his hopes and beliefs. During those hours together, when emotions and sensibilities were heightened by the threat of impending death, the bond between the two men grew into a mutual love and respect. Clive also drove to Walnut Grove to make an initial investigation of the case and begin the task of drawing up more than 40 affidavits from potential character witnesses and the lawyers who had previously been employed on the case. Eventually, about six days before the execution date, after an all-night stint working on the case, Clive was able to file a petition seeking a stay of execution from the Mississippi Supreme Court. In it he raised a number of new points, the majority of them based on legal technicalities or constitutional law.

Chief among these points was the fact that Edward's trial lawyers had been, in legal terms, 'ineffective' in the way they represented him. This argument had not been put forward before as until this point Jess Brown had continued to represent Edward and was therefore not about to claim his own ineffectiveness as a reason for overturning the sentence. Clive also alleged that the conduct of the trial had shown 'purposeful racial discrimination' in violation of the US Constitution. And, in what Clive was later to admit was an eleventh-hour legal manoeuvre, he also put forward psychiatric reports to show that Edward could not now be executed because he was currently insane. The Mississippi Supreme Court rejected all these arguments, and many more based on legal technicalities, on 18th May.

While waiting for the state supreme court to decide on his petition, Clive also took Edward's case to the district court in Jackson. He put forward the 34 affidavits he had collected from people who were prepared to testify to Edward's good character and who said they would have given evidence on his behalf at the original trial had they been asked to do so. He also persuaded Jess Brown and Firnist Alexander to sign sworn statements detailing their inexperience of the law concerning capital murder charges, the problems they faced in conducting the trial under intimidating circumstances, and the ways in which they had misinterpreted the law to Edward's disadvantage. The district court turned down the appeal on 19th May.

That same day, with only hours to go before Edward was due to die in the gas chamber, Clive went to a federal court, the Fifth Circuit Court of Appeals, to seek a stay of execution to allow time for his arguments on Edward's behalf to be given further consideration. The court concluded in a lengthy written statement which re-stated many of the arguments of the district court, that 'Johnson's present counsel have failed to raise any new or different issues which indicate that Johnson failed to receive a basically fair trial of his guilt and punishment'. It ruled also that errors, mistakes or omissions made by the lawyers who had previously represented Edward had not deprived him of a fair trial. Edward's plea was refused.

There was only one court left, the highest court in the land, the US Supreme Court. Clive heard the news of its decision as he waited with Edward in his cell on Death Row the night the black man was due to die. The answer, again, was no. It was of no comfort that two of the seven Supreme Court judges disagreed with the majority verdict and argued that Edward should be granted a stay of execution. There were no legal avenues left. The last door clanged shut shortly before midnight on 19th May when the news came through that the Governor of Mississippi had refused a plea for mercy.

So it was that Edward's young life ended in the dark hours of 20th May, 1987. He had been born deprived and died deprived. He had been the victim of hardship and adversity throughout his 26 years. He could never have hoped to be more than a second-class citizen. For the last few years of his life, in Parchman Penitentiary, he had not even been that.

But throughout it all, Edward retained that essential requisite of humanity, the ability to love and be loved. He had been nurtured in the love of his grandparents, aunts and cousins, and that love was still with him on the night he died. So, too, was Clive's love for the young black man, whom he had fought so desperately to save. And so, too, was the love of his fellow prisoner, Sam Johnson, who, from the depths of the inhumanity of Death Row, gave to Edward this moving epitaph:

'Edward was indeed many things to many people. A black child caught up in Mississippi's racist system, he was one of the many Americans who are afforded few, if any, of the many rights constitutionally guaranteed them. Yet, to me, 'Chui' [as he was known] was a man who rose above his tragedies and environment. He was a Christian who daily gave real meaning to love ... He was the 'kid brother' I never had.

When a good person dies, it is not their words but their deeds that are remembered. I loved and love 'Chui' for the person he truly was. If you had known him, you would have loved him too. I grieve for him. I grieve also, as he did during his life here on Death Row, for the Trest family and the pain they suffered and will always feel upon remembering their loved one. I grieve for 'Chui's' family and their pain. I pray for both families. I pray, too, that all who haven't will learn how to forgive. If we cannot forgive, we cannot expect to be forgiven.

Was the death of Edward Earl Johnson the death of a murderer? I think not. The murderer is the death penalty. It sits patiently, with its sardonic grin, waiting to touch you directly or indirectly through a family member or a loved one. No, the murderer did not die; the murderer lives.'

Nine

Who Killed Marshal Trest?

Sam's words, written after Edward was killed in the Mississippi gas chamber, were an indictment of the death penalty. 'The murderer lives,' he wrote. Those who legislate in favour of the death penalty, the people who carry out the laws, who oversee the procedures, who pull the switches or press the buttons, who strap the condemned man in the chair, are as much murderers as the person condemned to die; the vast majority of the population of the United States, who are overwhelmingly in favour of execution, are passive killers. By giving their approval through the ballot box to capital punishment, these people are also culpable of the worst crime known to the human race, the taking away of another man's life.

'The murderer lives.' Clive Stafford Smith would agree with that. But for him the words held a double meaning. For Clive, intent upon unearthing the truth about what really happened the night Marshal Jake Trest was killed in Walnut Grove, the murderer lived, not only in the figurative sense that Sam had intended when he wrote the words, but also literally in the shape of the unknown man who had pulled the trigger that fateful June night and was probably still alive and walking the streets somewhere in the United States. For, if Edward did not kill the marshal, who did?

That was the question to which Clive wanted the answer when he went to Walnut Grove soon after Edward's execution to start his own investigation into the murder, eight years after the event. If he could answer that question and find the evidence to prove it, he would be able to demonstrate to the world and to the people of the United States in particular, that an innocent man had had his life taken away from him in the Mississippi gas chamber. 'Most people who have doubts about the death penalty do so because they think an innocent person could be killed,' Clive believes. 'This is the single most emotive issue. It is not for man to claim omniscience, and the execution of the innocent is inevitable. Capital punishment was abolished in England after the true killer confessed to a crime for which another had been convicted. Unfortunately the confession came after the innocent man's neck had been broken by the hangman's noose.'

Clive went to Walnut Grove to search out the truth. It was a brave and courageous act to even venture into this small community on such a mission. Inevitably he would arouse deep hostility among the 400 or so people living within the town boundaries. Most of them are white. They did not want to have this incident from the past, now dead and buried in the most literal sense, resurrected and re-examined once again under the legal microscope. They did not take kindly to an outsider poking his nose into what they considered to be their own affairs and perhaps pointing out their own wrong-doing. 'They do not want to admit they have made a mistake,' said Clive. 'They just want to forget. Justice is not important.'

Mississippi folk have a long tradition of rough dealing with people who think they know better than them. They gave short shrift to the liberals of the civil rights years and they are prepared to do the same today. The smart-looking sign the citizens of Walnut Grove have seen fit to erect on the outskirts of their town is little more than a cosmetic public-relations exercise. 'Walnut Grove, the small town with a big heart,' it reads in pristine lettering superimposed over a large red heart. 'Callous' would be a more appropriate description of the town's vital organ.

If Clive felt any hint of nervousness about his mission, however, he did not show it. He is used to danger. He courts it in his daily life, as he goes about his business of defending prisoners on Death Row. He carries two types of business cards. One identifies him for what he is, an attorney working for the Southern Prisoners' Defence Committee. The other merely states he works for a law centre. There are times when it is simply wiser to use the second card. He and his colleagues who work for the prisoners on Death Row have put themselves in the firing line, both figuratively and actually. They are standing up to be counted, the few among many, who are prepared to actively oppose the wishes of the vast majority. Most of the whites living in the Deep South would be glad to see Clive suffer the same fate as that intended for his clients. Most are unlikely to take the law into their own hands, but they would not grieve if someone else did. For the more rational and law-abiding citizens of America, those who would not normally resort to violence except in defence of their property, Clive's legal mantle gives him a certain amount of security. But it gives little protection from the bullet of a Klansman or crazed extremist in a land where killing is just another way of solving a problem.

On one of the walls of his Atlanta office, Clive has given pride of place to a newspaper cutting which sums up his situation in four brief words. 'America's Most Hated Lawyer,' it proclaims in bold black type above a photograph of Clive at work in his office. The article is taken from a Canadian, not an American, newspaper. It takes another outsider to spell out the truth to a nation that prefers to disguise unpleasantness with a plethora of euphemisms. Clive is rather pleased with the headline. He likes the *bête noir* role he has created for himself. Danger is something he shakes off with a laugh and a shrug of his shoulders. He is dismissive of the possibility that his own life may be under threat. 'I don't mind if they shoot me,' he says. 'My death might do more to end the death penalty than anything else I can do.' For one who works so hard to save the lives of other people, he is remarkably cavalier about his own. He does not dream of adopting a low profile and keeping his head down, rather the reverse. He takes an active part in the politics of capital punishment and race in the Deep South. He attends civil rights meetings and anti-Klan rallies where his height and the colour of his skin make him an easy target for would-be assassins. He has been shot at once but it is not an incident he chooses to dramatise. 'Just some crazy guy shooting wildly,' is how he describes the event. 'He wasn't shooting at me. It was just rather difficult to explain the bullet holes in the car to the hire company.'

Indeed Clive seems to thrive on danger. Its presence drives the adrenalin through his body, providing him with the energy reserves he needs to maintain his punishing schedule. He likes the excitement and he likes his work. 'I am not a martyr to the cause. I enjoy it,' he says. Sometimes he seems just like a big kid who gets kicks from what he does. Sometimes, just occasionally, it is apparent that he is still a young man, only just into his third decade. But as a rule he demonstrates a maturity beyond his years. The relaxed, almost reckless manner which he presents to the world may sometimes seem irresponsible, but it is not so. It is his way of coping with the stresses and strains that he faces. It is also one of the weapons in his armoury. 'The best thing to do is to laugh at them,' he says of the society which hates him. 'It irritates them.'

Clive went to Walnut Grove to look for a murderer, but he also went to look for the truth. He felt in his heart that Edward was innocent of the crime for which he died, but, as a lawyer, he knows that nothing is certain. The only thing of which he was absolutely sure was that the truth had not come out at Edward's trial. He did not know what his inquiries would reveal. It was even possible that he might learn something that would implicate Edward in the murder. If he did, he would have to be able to cope with it. Facing that fact took a different sort of courage.

The young lawyer's first objective was to clear up some of the mysteries surrounding the trial itself. Clive had been puzzled by the strange events surrounding the black juror, Mrs Eddie Leflore, who had maintained so strenuously that she was able to read and write, despite all evidence to the contrary. Why did she persist in denying the fact that she could not read, when her admission might have been grounds for the granting of a new trial with the possibility that a different verdict might be reached?

The answer was common knowledge among the black community in the area, as Clive and a legal colleague were quick to discover when they made a few inquiries. Mrs Leflore had a son called Howard, who had been convicted of manslaughter at Carthage Courthouse in April, 1980, a few months before Edward's trial. Howard Leflore had been sentenced to five years in prison in the Misissippi State Penitentiary at Parchman. Another son, Ollie Leflore, had been convicted of grand larceny around the same time. Both these young men were in Carthage jail awaiting transfer to Parchman Penitentiary at the time their mother was sitting on the jury trying Edward for his life. According to the black community, Mrs Leflore was left in little doubt about the treatment that would be meted out to her sons if she did or said anything that would provide Edward's lawyers with a legal loophole. Her co-operation appeared to be rewarded. The two Leflore men did not have to serve their sentences in the rigorous environment of the Mississippi State Penitentiary. They were allowed to remain in local jails and were released early.

And Mrs Leflore was not the only black juror who had good reason to be prejudiced against Edward. In May, 1979, a young black man called Robert Ficklin had also appeared in the Leake County Court charged with murder. He had been found guilty of manslaughter and sentenced to twelve years' imprisonment in the Mississippi State Penitentiary. His father, Vardaman Ficklin, was also one of the twelve people chosen to sit on the jury that was to decide Edward's fate. Another son, Edward Ficklin, was also in prison serving a sentence for selling marijuana.

These four men, the Ficklins and the Leflores had all been sentenced in Leake County Court by Judge Marcus Gordon. The prosecution cases had been conducted by the District Attorney. All the potential jurors summoned for Edward's trial had, before being chosen for the jury, been asked to declare in court whether there was any reason why they might be prejudiced one way or another in the forthcoming trial. One of the questions specifically asked by the District Attorney had been: 'Have any members of your immediate family or close personal friends that you know of been involved recently in the trial of a case in circuit court, whether it be civil or criminal?' Several people responded to the question, but Mr Ficklin and Mrs Leflore said nothing. Jess Brown and Firnist Alexander knew nothing of the true facts about these two black people. Their lack of local knowledge had prohibited them from objecting to the presence of Mrs Leflore and Mr Ficklin on the jury. But the information was well known among the people of Leake County and, as Clive discovered, readily available. A study of the Leake County Court records was enough to establish the facts. The implications were self-evident. 'The black people on the jury were old. They couldn't read or write or stand up to the whites. There was a lot of fear. Older people are more afraid because they remember the old days,' black activist Winson Hudson was to tell Clive when he visited her in her Carthage home. Clive knows the situation well. He has come across cases where black jurors are so intimidated by merely being on a jury that even though their names are recorded for all to see, they have denied being jurors when Clive has approached them after the trial. He knows the pressure that can be brought to bear on vulnerable black jurors in racist Mississippi.

But this new information about the composition of the jury did not help to prove Edward innocent and it did not answer any of the questions about what had happened to Marshal Trest the night he was killed.

While he was in Leake County Courthouse examining the records, Clive therefore decided to have a closer look at the two weapons that the prosecution claimed had been used in the murder. He hoped he might be able to find a lead to the truth from a thorough investigation of some of the physical evidence that had been produced in court. Perhaps he might learn something from an examination of the weapons that had been used to kill the officer. It was yet another puzzling aspect of the case that there had been so little positive identification of the weapons during the trial, so little evidence to link them to Edward or indeed Marshal Trest. Items presented as exhibits in a trial are normally held in safe-keeping in the sheriff's office in the courthouse. But when Clive sought to inspect the guns there was nothing to see. They had vanished. All that remained were the brown paper bags in which they had been kept and three bullets. The police were unable or unwilling to provide any explanation. There was no way now in which Clive could check the serial numbers on the weapons or in any other way seek to identify them. It was impossible for Clive to attempt to link the guns to anybody else. He did not even have a precise description of the .25 that had been said to belong to Edward. Some people told him that the one introduced in court had a brown handle. Others said it was white. Some people said that Edward had owned a brown-handled gun. Others again said it was white. 'The evidence on the guns was totally confusing and confused,' said Clive. Any hope that the guns would reveal new information was doomed to failure. He could only theorise as to how Edward, in his confession, came to reveal the precise location of the Smith & Wesson. The most obvious answer was that it had been planted there, to be conveniently discovered by a passer-by. If Edward was innocent and knew nothing of the murder, he must have been told what to say in his confession. That would include being instructed where to say the gun could be found.

Clive's initial inquiries were leading nowhere. He was making little progress in his attempt to establish what had happened in Walnut Grove that night. The response from the white community to his polite inquiries was to shut the door in his face. The police refused to speak to him, either on or off the record. They would not discuss the case at all. His approaches to Joe Mack Thaggard had equally negative results. The man who helped to convict Edward is no longer sheriff of Leake County but he has remained in the area. Clive and a colleague tried to visit him at his luxury home with its row of five expensive cars parked in the driveway. But he got no further than the front doorstep. In answer to Clive's knock, Joe Mack Thaggard appeared at the door clad in his usual garb, including the 'shit-kicker' cowboy boots, and chewing his customary tobacco. 'He made us stand outside while he stood at the top of three steps leading up to a screened porch. Every few words he would get together a good glob and spit it out on the ground between us, as if to say what would happen if we approached any closer,' says Clive, describing the meeting. Phone calls to the house elicited the response that the former sheriff had nothing to say.

Miss Sally was equally uncommunicative. She still lives in the same house in Walnut Grove and Clive made several attempts to speak to her without success. The woman who answered his phone calls told him: 'Miss Sally is not here. Don't call back. I don't give a damn who you are.' Clive believes the speaker was Miss Sally herself. Her lodger at the time of the murder, Mr Carmen Dennis, is dead. He, the only other person who might have given evidence about the struggle between Miss Sally and her assailant, died shortly before the trial. No statement was ever read out or referred to. Whatever he might have had to say has never been heard and never will be.

The black community was more open to Clive's approaches but even so, there were barriers to be overcome. Edward had plenty of relatives and friends still living in the area, people who believed in his innocence and wished to help Clive. But it takes courage for a black person in Leake County to be seen to be helping a man such as Clive, a man seeking to prove that the wrong man was convicted of the murder of Marshal Trest. The fact that a dozen or more relatives and friends did confide in Clive is evidence of the strength of the belief among blacks in the area that Edward had been the victim of a gross injustice.

The black community told Clive that Edward could not have been the man who shot Marshal Trest as he was with several other people at the time of the murder. Much of their story was the same as that put forward in evidence at the trial as an alibi. Edward had been at a card game with friends and relatives which went on well into the early hours of the morning. The difference was that whereas at the trial the others who were present had put the time of Edward's departure at about 2.00 am, they now all said the game had gone on for longer, until well after 2.30 am when the shooting was said to have taken place. They could be absolutely sure about the time, they said, because Edward's car had been blocking in some of the other members of the party and they had had to ask him to move it before they could leave. Thelma Johnson, Edward's aunt, was particularly sure about the time because she had been trying to make her husband leave and take her home for some time because it was getting late.

If that was the case, why had they testified to a different time at the trial, Clive wanted to know? It seemed suspiciously convenient that everyone involved was now prepared to swear to a story that would indeed provide Edward with an alibi. The explanation, he was told, was that Edward's lawyers and the black community as a whole had been misled about the timing of the shooting. They thought the attack on Miss Sally had taken place shortly after 2.00 am as this was the time that had been reported in the media the day after the event. Brown and Alexander had prepared Edward's alibi, therefore, to cover the period around 2.00 am and had continued with this story despite the fact that during the trial the police had put the time at 2.30 am or later. It was the police that had first moved the time forward a good 30 minutes, and Edward's relatives were now only doing the same thing, Clive was led to believe. They could have done so during the trial if they had realised what was going on. Timing, it seemed, was somewhat moveable: it could be slid backwards and forwards at will.

Clive had reason to give some credence to the explanation. The prosecution evidence about the time of the attack had not been consistent during the trial. Miss Sally had said she knew she had been awakened about 2.25 am because she had looked at her clock and that was the time it showed. But she also volunteered the information that she always kept her clocks fast. Another witness who lived nearby and had been one of the first on the scene corroborated Miss Sally's testimony about the time, but she too had noted it from glancing at clocks in the house. Dr David Moody, the young, recently qualified doctor who, by a strange co-incidence worked for the sheriff's namesake, a Dr Thaggard, had been alerted in Carthage and recorded the time of his arrival in Walnut Grove at 2.25 am. It was written on his report of the incident which was presented as evidence in court. But when this was pointed out to him by Alexander, he told the jury that it was a mistake made by his secretary. He had, in fact, arrived at the scene at 3.00 am. The time of death, he said, occurred between 2.00 am and 3.00 am. He could not be more precise than that.

Another black woman, a cousin of Edward's called Mary Harris, gave Clive yet more information about that night and subsequent events. Edward did not go home after the card game, she said. He went to a pool hall several miles from Walnut Grove. She had been there herself and seen the young man. She had even gone to Carthage courthouse during the trial to try and give evidence on Edward's behalf, but she had been met at the door by Sheriff Joe Mack Thaggard and told to go away. 'He said they did not need me,' she told Clive.

But whatever Clive thought of the new information he was given about Edward's alibi, he knew it was not the sort of evidence that would stand up in court. These people were all friends and relatives of Edward. It was only natural they would do their best to give him a cast-iron alibi. They were also talking about an event which had occurred eight years before. Most people cannot be precise about what they were doing eight days before, let alone eight years. 'People can convince themselves that something is true if they talk about it enough. Eight years is a long time to talk about something,' Clive says.

There were times during his visits to Walnut Grove, visits which had to be squeezed into an already full timetable, when Clive felt that he was never going to come any closer to the facts of what had happened. Sometimes, it seemed to him that the truth had been buried as deeply as had been the case many years before when the Philadephia freedom riders had been murdered in the neighbouring county. His conviction that Edward was innocent was as strong as ever, but he had nothing concrete to show for the time he had spent re-opening this can of worms. Several months had passed since Edward's death and he was still no further forward. He needed some assistance with his investigation. That help was to come from a surprising source, from his own compatriots in England.

At the time of Edward's execution a television crew had been making a documentary film about the death penalty in the USA. The BBC producer Paul Hamann had long wanted to make a film which would illustrate the true barbarity of the death penalty. He had been advised by nearly everyone he spoke to that, to be effective, the film must be made at the time of execution, when the sentence was about to be carried out. Only then, he was told, could the full horror be shown. He had approached several states in America as long before as 1984 requesting permission to bring a film crew on to Death Row for an execution. The Mississippi authorities had agreed in principle. But Paul had to wait three years before he received a phone call from the state telling him to bring his team over as an execution was likely to take place soon at Parchman Penitentiary. The man scheduled to die was Edward Johnson. The crew stayed with Edward until less than an hour before his execution and the results of their visit were shown on television in Britain and throughout the world in a moving documentary called '14 Days in May'.

Paul Hamann had been deeply touched by Edward and his plight. He had arrived at the prison not knowing what to expect and had met a quietly spoken, articulate and gentle young man. He was well aware of the prison officers' old adage that there are few guilty men in prison. Most will protest their innocence. But his cycnicism had vanished during the three weeks before Edward's death, spent almost continuously in the young black man's company. In common with fellow Death Row prisoners and many of the penitentiary staff, Paul Hamann, too, became convinced that a gross miscarriage of justice was about to take place.

He formed a close relationship with Edward. 'I became his friend,' he said two years later in his BBC office in London. 'I saw Edward every day and we became extremely close. So many people will tell you they are innocent. Edward was the one person that everyone else said was innocent, even right-wing prison warders. I came to realise there was something different about this young man.' Paul came to know the condemned man's story well, and so convinced did he become of Edward's innocence, that he eventually abandoned his detached, professional role as an observer and interceded on the black man's behalf only hours before his death, personally telephoning the Governor of Mississippi to plead for clemency. Edward's death moved him more deeply than almost anything else he had encountered during his years as a documentary film maker, years which had placed him in many traumatic situations in strife-torn countries such as Namibia and Northern Ireland. 'For a year after his death there was not a day that I did not think of Edward. I am not over it now,' says Paul who confesses openly that he has shed many tears for the young man.

Like Clive, Paul decided that Edward's execution was not the end. He too felt that the true story needed to be told. That night in May 1987, at Parchman Death Row, he decided that he would return with his film crew to Mississippi and document as much as was possible of the real Walnut Grove story.

The two Englishmen, Clive and Paul, had also become friends during those fraught three weeks before Edward's death. Their relationship grew after Paul returned to London and, as Clive continued his mission on one side of the Atlantic, thousands of miles away Paul made his own arrangements to go back to the small Mississippi community. Thus it was that early in 1988 the BBC producer and his film crew returned to the scene of the murder of Marshal Jake Trest to join Clive in his attempts to unearth the truth and record the results of that investigation for posterity in a second film that was later to be seen in millions of homes around the world under the title 'The Journey'.

With the assistance of the BBC team Clive eventually made the breakthrough he needed. The lawyer had been sure from the start that there were many people in the Walnut Grove area who knew a great deal more than they were willing to reveal at first. Clive's problem was to persuade them to part with this information. He and the film crew had first-hand experience of the intimidation that could be brought to bear on people to stop the investigation proceeding. Cars were driven at the team in the street, people refused to serve them in restaurants, extreme action was threatened against any minor infringement of the law such as illegal parking. Most people in the area would not speak because they were frightened to do so. A few might well incriminate themselves if they did. The closed door began to open slowly when members of the black community were asked if they knew anyone who fitted the description that Miss Sally was said to have given of her assailant immediately after the incident. Was there anyone in the area at the time who fitted the description of 'low and chunky with chin beards'? Was there anyone who looked like that who might have committed the murder?

The answer, it seemed, was yes. There had been a man who fitted that description who had lived on the outskirts of Walnut Grove. He had left the area shortly after the murder and had not been seen since. That, of course, did not make him a potential murderer. But there were some black people who were brave enough to give Clive a clue as to why the man might have killed Marshal Trest. They obviously knew a great deal more than they were prepared to tell Clive, especially in front of the television cameras, but the clue lay in the word 'drugs'. It was commonly thought, Clive discovered, that drug dealing had been taking place in Walnut Grove around the time of the murder.

Some detective work established that the man who fitted the description was now living in Alabama, not far from the Mississippi state line. Clive and the film crew decided to take the bull by the horns. They would go to Alabama and speak to the man who, according to the black community of Walnut Grove, could be the murderer of Marshal Trest. Even Clive was daunted by the prospect of confronting a man who might have killed in cold blood once and could possibly do so again. If he was indeed a dangerous man, a murderer, was it not extremely likely that Clive would meet the same fate as Marshal Trest? 'I was a little worried about it,' he now admits with typical understatement and a wry smile.

But Clive could see little alternative. The truth about the events in Walnut Grove that had led to Edward's death, could well lie with this man. Clive was driven on by the need to know. Accompanied by the BBC film crew, he made the journey to the Alabaman town and the shabby former motel where the man was now living with his wife.

It was his wife who answered Clive's anxious knock at the door. Her husband, was not at home, she said. He was expected back later that night. For eight hours Clive and the film crew waited in their cars around the corner from the building, watching for the man's return. Eventually their patience was rewarded. As they spotted him returning home, Clive and the others left their cars and approached him as he was about to enter the building.

It is hard to say who was more frightened by the meeting. Clive and the film crew had had plenty of time to imagine in dreadful detail the reaction they might receive from this man, who was known to be a Vietnam War veteran and to carry a powerful gun. The suspect, on the other hand, was taken by surprise. The film of the meeting, as shown later on BBC television, revealed that the former Walnut Grove resident was as scared as anyone present to be accosted on his doorstep by a group of white men, one of whom announced himself to be the lawyer representing the interests of Edward Johnson.

It was several minutes before the man was composed enough to answer any questions coherently. When he did calm down and listen to Clive's explanation that he was investigating the death of Marshal Trest, he agreed that the group could come into the house to discuss the matter further. During the course of the interview, which was included in the television film, he became increasingly confident, almost cocksure. Yes, he had known Edward Johnson, he said. No, he did not think he should have died. There are many other people he would rather see dead. But he did not crack when Clive directly accused him of being the murderer of Marshal Trest. He denied it with a strange good humour, almost challenging Clive to prove it if he could. It was an anticlimactic end to hours and days of tension for the young lawyer.

Clive could not prove that Edward was not the killer then, and he cannot prove it today. But he knows much more than can ever be said publicly. What he needs is the conclusive evidence that would provide a watertight case in court. He is almost certain who did kill Marshal Trest, and why, but he cannot say so – yet. He believes that more than one person was involved in the murder, that there was a conspiracy to cover it up. Edward had been picked as the fall guy. But for the world at large the question still remains: 'Who killed Marshal Trest?' Clive, however, has not given up the fight. It is not in his nature to do so. He continues to visit the man in Alabama when he is passing through the area and the two have established an unlikely sparring relationship, a relationship that has become a game of cat and mouse. There are several other people in Walnut Grove to whom Clive would still like to talk, and whom he has made several attempts to see, but so far they have eluded him.

Over the months Clive has become extremely fond of Edward's grandmother, Jessie Mae, and goes to see her as often as he can. He has great admiration for the old lady, now a widow well into her eighties, and living every day with the heartbreak that Edward's death has caused her. She too has never lost her faith in Edward and has her own beliefs about what really happened that night in Walnut Grove. But she keeps her thoughts and feelings to herself. It would be unwise to do otherwise. 'Folk treat me good and still treat me nice,' she says. That is important in the small community where she lives. Her position is no different from the white man she knows of who probably witnessed some of the events yet refused to give vital evidence on Edward's behalf saying: 'I have got to live here.' Jessie Mae knows that many people did not tell the truth at Edward's trial but she holds her own counsel. When she sees Miss Sally, as she inevitably does from time to time, the two women behave as though nothing has happened. 'She passed by here the other day and waved at me.

I waved at her,' says Jessie Mae, with a sad, private smile that speaks as much as her words. 'If I was Miss Sally I would not have a clear enough conscience to speak to me and wave to me.' She supports Clive in his quest to prove Edward innocent. 'It will not help him but it might help other people,' she says. One day both she and Clive hope that he will have enough time to find the concrete evidence he needs to bring the case to court again. It may not be in the old lady's lifetime.

In the meantime, though, Clive continues to live at his frenetic pace, trying to cope with the demands made upon him by the many men who are still alive on Death Row, men who still have something to hope for. 'I pray for the dead and fight like hell for the living,' is how Clive describes his life today, quoting a twentieth-century guru. That means fighting for men like Edward's friend, Sam Johnson, waiting in his cell on Death Row. Edward is not forgotten. Sam lives on.

Ten

Sam

'I still can't believe this has happened to me,' says Sam Johnson, as he sits behind the bars of the visiting area on Mississippi Death Row. 'I keep pinching myself and hope I will wake up.' He shakes his head in sad disbelief. Then he looks up and a broad infectious smile lights up his face. 'I ain't got nothing but bruises so far,' he grins ruefully, inviting the visitor to share in his humour.

There does not seem much to laugh about. It is a wet, grey day in Mississippi. In the narrow, shabby corridor that passes as a visiting room on Parchman Death Row, the steady dripping of the rain can be heard as it seeps through a hole in the roof into a strategically placed bucket on the floor. Sam Johnson has been brought into the visiting area in shackles. He is weighed down with iron: his wrists are handcuffed and attached to a chain around his waist so that he cannot lift his hands above chest level; he wears leg irons on his ankles, restricting his walk to a slow shuffle. He is forced to speak to his visitors through steel bars covered in close-knit wire mesh designed to prevent all physical contact. The brick building which houses the execution chamber where he is scheduled to die is only a few short yards away.

Yet Sam Johnson is not a broken man. Despite his circumstances, he has maintained his dignity and humanity. He likes to laugh and talk and joke. He is witty, intelligent, and good company. The sheer strength of his personality overcomes the physical circumstances in which he is confined. At the end of visiting time, as he gets up to return to his Death Row cell, he holds up his manacled hands. 'They have got me in handcuffs,' he says, 'but they have not got me in prison.'

The state of Mississippi thinks otherwise. Like Edward, Sam Johnson is also a vicious killer, it says. He too is destined to die in the gas chamber at Parchman Penitentiary. Depending on the success or failure of his legal appeals against the sentence, he has another two or three years to live. It is just possible he may win a reprieve. At the worst it may only be months before he is strapped into the chair in the execution chamber to choke to death on the poisonous cyanide fumes.

Sam is 46 years old and black. He was born and raised in the North, in Rochester, New York State, a world apart from the inbred racialism of the South. Unlike Edward, he was brought up to believe himself the equal of any man. 'I have never felt like a slave,' he says. 'That is because I was brought up in the North. I have never felt that I am less than other people, but this mentality exists here today. We are regarded as inferior. Some of the guards here think that black people are less than animals. That attitude took hold of Edward towards the end and made a slave of him.'

Sam is a man who has experienced much of the world; he has travelled widely within the United States, and has a variety of jobs behind him. He has been a husband but is now divorced, and is a father and grandfather. He has been a prisoner on Death Row since 1982 when he was convicted of killing a white policeman near the small Mississippi town of Collins, about a hundred miles south of Jackson.

In 1981, on New Year's Eve, he was driving north from New Orleans together with three other black men when the car was stopped by a Mississippi Highway Patrolman. Officer Billy Langham, who was on duty alone, asked to see Sam's driving licence. When he admitted he did not have one, the officer ordered the four men out of the car and made them line up by the police vehicle. He was suspicious of their reasons for being in the area and started to search the empty car. The patrolman's misgivings were well-founded. Sam and his three companions were on their way to Collins to try and cash some forged cheques at a bank in the town. As the policeman leaned into the car to look under the seats, one of the black men left the side of the police car and plunged a butcher's knife into the officer's back. Billy Langham staggered back, blood streaming from his wound, and attempted to grapple with his attacker. There was a scuffle involving some of the others. Then they made for their car, climbed in and as they were doing so, one of them grabbed the officer's gun and shot him. The whole incident was over within a matter of seconds. The four men made their escape in the car, abandoned it in Collins and transferred to another stolen vehicle. They were stopped at a roadblock about ten miles from the town.

Murder charges were brought against Sam and two of his companions, Otis Fairley and Charles Montgomery. The fourth man, Anthony Fields, turned state's evidence and was convicted of a lesser charge. At Sam's trial, Fields told the jury that Sam had stabbed the policeman and then ordered Montgomery to shoot him. The policeman had found the knife in the front of the car where Sam had been sitting, Fields said. Langham had placed it on the roof of the police car within easy reach of the men standing by the vehicle while he continued his search of their car. Sam had taken hold of the knife and attacked the patrolman. Fairley and Montgomery were found guilty of murder and sentenced to life imprisonment. Sam was sentenced to die. From his prison cell he protests his innocence. It was Fields, not he, who stabbed and then shot the policeman, he says.

There is no denying that Sam was present at the time of the murder of Billy Langham, nor that he and his companions were engaged in criminal activities. Sam is the first to admit that he has led a far from blameless life. He is no stranger to prison. He is a petty crook with a long list of convictions for forgery behind him. But that, says Sam, does not make him a murderer. 'I cannot justify the things I have done in my life,' he said. 'But I am not a violent man. I am far from being a saint and even further from being a murderer.'

Sam's story of what happened that New Year's Eve goes like this. He had met up with the other three men in New Orleans, where he was living at the time with his wife and step-daughter, and they had decided to make some easy money by cashing the forged cheques. He knew Montgomery and Fairley but had never met Fields before. The latter was Fairley's first cousin and the two men came originally from Collins. They said they had contacts there who would help them to cash the cheques.

When the four men were stopped and ordered out of the car, Fields did not go over to the police car with the others. Instead he produced a knife, which Sam did not know he possessed, and stabbed the patrolman in the back. Sam discovered later that Fields knew the patrolman and was aware that he had been responsible for killing a black man a few months earlier. He believes that Fields stabbed the policeman because he was frightened that their lives would also be in danger.

When Sam saw what was happening he rushed over to the car and tried to stop Fields. All three men were involved in the ensuing struggle during which Sam's hand was badly cut in two places. In panic Sam and the other two men clambered into the car to escape. As they were doing so they heard a gunshot. Fields then got into the car and told Sam to 'drive'. 'I was so panic filled at this time I couldn't do anything but what he told me,' said Sam. 'None of us at this time knew whether he still had the knife or the gun and all of us were panic filled.'

Sam drove to a deserted part of Collins as directed by Fields and they abandoned the car. Montgomery and Sam then tried to run off but, being strangers to the town, they had no idea of where they were going. Fields stole another car, drove after the two men and told them to get in. They set off again but were soon stopped at the roadblock where the police opened fire on the car. 'It was God's grace that we weren't killed at the roadblock,' says Sam. 'Fields knew several officers who were at the roadblock and told them that Montgomery and I killed the officer. We were almost beaten to death. Fear isn't the correct word for what I was that day, but it's the only word that I know that can come close to describing the feelings that were within me then.'

The four men were taken to the local jail where, Sam says, he was threatened by the authorities. He was not allowed to see a lawyer for several weeks after his arrest, and was under constant intimidation. He soon realised that he was going to take the blame for the murder of the policeman, but there was nothing he could do to help himself. Fields and Fairley had relatives in Collins, who were able to support them, but Sam had no-one to turn to. The police called him a Yankee nigger, he says, a double term of abuse in southern Mississippi. As an outsider, he was the obvious one to take the rap.

There are several points that cast doubt on the story as told by Fields. Billy Langham had been murdered in broad daylight on one of the state's busiest highways. Many people saw the killing as they passed by in their cars. Several stopped when they realised what was happening. They also gave evidence in court during Sam's trial about what they had seen. The only man to be identified by the witnesses was Fields. Nobody remembered seeing a man of Sam's description stabbing or shooting the policeman.

And what of the weapon, Sam asks? Is it likely that an experienced police officer like Billy Langham would have casually left such a lethal weapon as the butcher's knife lying on the roof of the patrol car within easy reach of these four suspicious characters? It is an insult to the officer to think that he would, Sam says. The true story is that Fields had the knife in his possession all the time and Langham was unaware of it. He would never have turned his back on the men if he had known they were armed. In support of his story, Sam also points to the fact that the cuts on his hand were so placed that they could not have been made by someone using the knife as a weapon.

But despite the unanswered questions and lack of conclusive evidence to indicate that Sam had been the man to murder the patrolman, he was convicted of the crime and sentenced to die. Sam says he never stood a chance at his trial. He claims that, like Edward, whom he was to befriend in Parchman Penitentiary, he was the victim of racism, intimidation and incompetence.

Clive took over the handling of Sam's case about four years after the murder. He has investigated the background and has evidence to back up some of the black man's claims.

Fearing rightly that Sam would not receive a fair trial because of the publicity the murder had already received, and the sense of outrage among local people at the killing of a white policeman, the attorneys representing Sam asked for the case to be heard in a different county. It was agreed that it would be, but unfortunately they unwittingly agreed that the trial should be held in an area that is one of the strongholds of the Ku Klux Klan, Pike County which borders Louisiana.

Sam has been fighting to prove his innocence ever since he arrived at Parchman Penitentiary. After the trial he changed his lawyer. The new lawyer appealed for the case to be re-tried, listing a plethora of reasons for so doing, but this request was eventually turned down by the Mississippi Supreme Court in 1985. One of the points raised by the lawyer had been that the trial attorneys had waived their right to object to the District Attorney's closing argument until after he had finished and when the jury was no longer present. It meant that the DA was in a position to sway the jury with statements which, had the defence objected, would normally have been over-ruled by the judge. The Supreme Court judges ruled that the defence attorneys' action was 'quite illogical and extreme and places the state in a Catch 22 situation'. But they could not allow that the DA's closing speech provided grounds for a re-trial because the defence had not objected at the time and allowed the trial judge to correct the situation. 'To allow defence counsel to argue at conclusion of argument, to which no objection has been made, he is then entitled to a mis-trial is not only inviting error, but also preventing the trial judge from taking the one step he could have taken to remove the possibility of prejudice,' the Supreme Court ruled. The judges also refused to grant a new trial based on the fact that the court had refused to grant funds for witnesses from the North to attend the trial to testify on Sam's behalf; nor was it relevant that the others convicted of murder had been given life sentences and not the death penalty. The court also said that Sam could not now complain that previous convictions had been used against him in court as he had not objected at the time. There was evidence, the judges agreed, to show that Fields had been less than the innocent bystander he claimed to be, but it was up to the jury, not the judges, to weigh up that evidence.

Shortly after the Mississippi Supreme Court ruling, Clive agreed to take over Sam's case. The black man was delighted. He knew Clive to be a dedicated and clever lawyer. 'Clive has done more to fight the death penalty than anyone I have met,' says Sam. 'Other lawyers do not have zeal and dedication as great as Clive's. They will not go into any kind of depth to bring the truth to light. All of the guys here, they all want Clive. He thinks so sincerely and wants to help.' Sam has also been deeply impressed with the way in which Clive has continued to fight for Edward after his death. 'There are very few who would have gone on as he has done with Edward Earl,' he said. 'I admire and respect him. He is a sharp individual, a beautiful individual.'

Clive is fond of Sam too, although the relationship is of a different intensity to the one he had with Edward. Clive loved Edward. Sam, he sees as an extremely likeable rogue. 'Edward really was a genuine innocent in both senses of the word,' says Clive. 'Not only did he not commit the murder, he was naïve as well. Sam is totally different. He is a super guy. I really like him. But he is one of the world's conmen. He is a nice crook. He is not a cardboard, one-dimensional goody-goody character. He is a good forger. But I don't think he would do anyone in.'

The relationship is not always a smooth one. Such is Sam's determination to prove his innocence, that he is not always prepared to take his lawyer's advice and sit back and wait. Sam maintains consistently that he is not a murderer. 'I keep battling because I do not have the burden of guilt weighing on my shoulders,' he says. Clive, on the other hand, is hopeful that he will be able to get Sam's death sentence overturned but is less sure that he will be able to prove him innocent, not because of lack of evidence to do so, but because of the way the legal system operates. It will take a re-trial to prove Sam did not commit the murder, as the American appeal courts usually do not choose to consider questions of guilt or innocence. But Sam is not content to fight for life imprisonment. He spends as many hours as he can in the prison law library and has become a self-taught mine of information on the American legal system. As a result, he has taken to filing his own petitions in court when he thinks he knows better than his lawyers. Clive would rather he did not do so, but understands the frustration and helplessness that the black man feels as he sits alone on Death Row. 'Filing his own petitions may help him psychologically but does not always help him legally,' says Clive. 'I have threatened to go and break his neck if he continues,' the lawyer adds with a laugh. 'Old Sam gets on his horse and starts galloping and throws the whole thing into disarray.'

The main street, Walnut Grove, close to where Marshal Jake Trest was murdered

City Hall, Walnut Grove, where Edward was first questioned about the murder

Clive Stafford Smith at Edward Johnson's grave

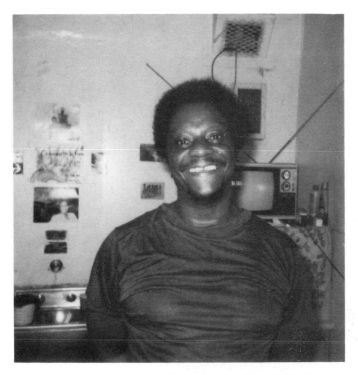

A polaroid photograph of Sam Johnson, taken in his cell

The Death Row complex within Parchman Penitentiary

Leo Edwards, who was executed at Parchman Penitentiary in June 1989

Sam's hopes of freedom have been raised since the summer of 1988 when Clive, together with colleagues from a large New York law firm, won a major victory on his behalf in the US Supreme Court. Its decision temporarily removed the threat of death hanging over Sam, and was also potentially significant for many other prisoners. It is destined to become a text-book case. The ruling came about after Clive and the New York lawyers challenged the validity of the previous conviction which had been used by the prosecution at Sam's trial to prove there were enough aggravating circumstances to warrant the death penalty. During the original trial, one of the major reasons put forward by the District Attorney for sentencing Sam to death was that he was an habitually violent man. Samuel Johnson deserved to die, the DA repeatedly told the jury, because he had a previous conviction for assault and attempted rape.

It was true. In 1963, while a young man, Sam had been charged and convicted of the crime in a New York State court. Sam had often tried to tell his other lawyers that the conviction was not worth the paper it was written on. But it was not until Clive took on the case that his protestations were taken seriously and investigations were started to ascertain the circumstances surrounding the conviction.

The incident which led to the charge had taken place in Rochester. Sam, then aged about 20, had returned home after leaving the US Air Force which he had joined from high school. He and a friend had been for a night out and were in high spirits when they saw a prostitute on a street corner. They pulled over and she got into the car. Sam said he would pay her $50. The woman soon discovered that neither of the two men had any money. She left the car angrily, noted the licence number and reported an attempted rape to the police. What the two young men had seen as rather a joke, albeit a bad one, had taken on more serious implications. Sam served a year in prison for the alleged offence.

When Clive discovered the flimsy basis for the conviction, he sought the help of the New York attorneys and together they lodged an appeal on Sam's behalf with the New York Court of Appeals. It reversed the conviction, ruling that it was invalid. But the Mississippi Supreme Court refused to accept that the fact that Sam's previous conviction was now null and void made any difference to his case. In a ruling that highlighted the divisions between North and South, the majority of judges on the Mississippi Supreme Court chose to ignore the judgement of the New York State Appeal Court. The fact that the Northern court had over-turned the conviction carried no weight with the Mississippi judges. Most of them were suspicious that the Northern court had only done so because it was opposed to the death penalty, which has been abolished in New York State.

One Mississippi judge disagreed with his colleagues. Justice James Robertson, the man who had at one time represented Edward Johnson, now spoke out on Sam's behalf. 'My colleagues,' he said, 'have "taken a swipe" at the New York court. I am not prepared to indulge in the cynical assumption that the New York court did less than its duty when it ordered Johnson's 1963 conviction vacated. I am confident the New York court has displayed no greater penchant for vacating 25-year-old convictions than this court.' The *New York Times* commented that the issue 'exposed the raw edges of the regional debate over capital punishment'.

Clive's next move was to take the argument to the US Supreme Court. It ruled unanimously in Sam's favour and overturned his death sentence. Sam was escstatic when he heard the news. 'Oh happy day,' he wrote to a friend. 'God, through the court's decision has shown me that He won't allow man to murder me, and knowing that He won't allow me to be murdered by man makes me know, even more than before, that He will cause these doors to be opened unto me. I know that I wasn't brought this far to be forsaken and I know that I will be free again.'

Clive's reaction was more cautious. The battle was not yet won. Sam remained on Death Row. His case must now go back to the Mississippi Supreme Court for re-sentencing. The outlook was not necessarily good. Immediately after the US Supreme Court ruling was announced, the Mississippi assistant attorney general said he would ask his state court to reimpose the death sentence. Clive feared that it might well do so. At the time of writing, Sam still waits on Death Row to hear his fate. Clive and the New York attorneys hope they will win him a re-sentencing trial at which his guilt or innocence could be raised.

The battle is far from over. Sam must continue his fight for both mental and physical survival on Death Row, in conditions to which a lesser man would already have succumbed. He knows it and it is hard. 'My lawyers tell me to be patient,' he said, 'but it is hard to have patience in here. Sometimes I feel that guilt or innocence ceases to matter. Now they are just focussing on whether I live or die. They will do the same thing to me as they did to Edward.' Sometimes even Sam's remarkable spirit and will to live are threatened by this knowledge and the environment in which he is imprisoned. 'At times I have depression which just knocks me to my knees. I have been so low that I have to reach up to touch the bottom,' he says. 'This is a death environment, an insane environment. Everything they do here is designed to oppress, suppress, depress and repress. Over the period of time it wears you away. We have conditions here like the prisoner-of-war camps. Some of the guards are racist. They call me New York nigger. This whole thing should be brought to the attention of the world. People are not aware it is like Nazi Germany. The only difference is of numbers. They prepare us to believe that death is preferable to these conditions. Edward felt like there was more on the other side than here, eventually. He had just given up. I try to maintain my manhood and dignity but it is very hard.'

Recently, however, Sam has been able to draw succour from an unexpected source. His isolation from the outside world has been breached, giving him the extra strength he needs to maintain his sanity and will to live. He has received vital moral and emotional support from many thousands of miles away. That support has come from a white man living in an English village, with whom Sam has formed a close and unique bond. Jan Arriens, who was born in England of Dutch parents, now lives with his wife and family in Whittlesford, near Cambridge, where he works from home as a freelance translator. He is an educated, cultured man with a degree from the University of Melbourne in Australia, where he spent much of his childhood, and a doctorate from the University of Cambridge. For several years he worked for the Australian diplomatic service in cities ranging from Kuala Lumpur to Brussels.

In 1987 he was one of many throughout the world who witnessed Edward's final days as depicted in Paul Hamann's documentary film '14 Days in May'. Jan was deeply moved by what he saw, so much so that he decided he must do something to try and help others still living on Death Row, some of whom had featured briefly in the film. 'They spoke with such extraordinary dignity, compassion and insight that I was prompted to write to them,' says Jan. It was a response from the heart. One of those he wrote to was Sam Johnson.

Within the closed environment of Death Row, mere letters take on an importance out of all proportion to that attached to a similar correspondence conducted in a free and open society. They are a link to the outside world. They provide a prisoner with the opportunity to express pent-up thoughts and emotions. They make a man feel human again. 'Thank you for caring enough to write,' Sam wrote back to Jan in a letter that spoke of his innocence of the crime for which he was convicted. 'I tell you about me and what has happened to me because if I am killed, I'll at least know that someone other than my family and someone outside of this country knows of the tragedy that was Sam Johnson.'

Sam's reply was the start of a long-distance correspondence that has established a remarkable rapport between the two men from such contrasting backgrounds. Jan writes to Sam several times a week. Sam responds as much as he is able, his letters curtailed only by practical necessities such as stamps and writing paper. The two men converse through their letters. They share their sadness and their happiness. They are at ease with each other. As Sam wrote to Jan in a letter about nine months after the correspondence started: 'We no longer have to "dare" to be ourselves with each other, we can just be ourselves with each other. Know what I mean? If so, a great big smile should just be starting to appear on that handsome face of yours. Gotcha!!! (smile). My Brother, things are going to get much better for the both of us and I just know this. In the very near future we are going to look back on all of this and smile at each other about it'.

The two men, the former forger and the former diplomat, write to each other as equals. 'To you and I there's no difference between us, and titles, colours or anything else make no difference to us at all,' wrote Sam. 'We ARE, and all of the extraneous stuff that's picked up along the road of life has no bearing or influence upon the closeness and unity that is OURS.' Sam picked up most of his education on the streets of Rochester, but he is a gifted man with intellectual abilities far beyond his formal qualifications. During his years on Death Row he has put his time to good use, reading widely on many and varied subjects. He is a natural writer. Jan has opened up for Sam a world he had never before experienced. In his letters to the man in the Cambridgeshire village he reveals his innermost soul, and in so doing paints a picture of the daily existence facing those awaiting execution – life on Death Row. In one letter he wrote:

'For the first year or so I was filled to the brim with pure hatred over what had happened to me. Losing all that I had and everyone who I loved filled me so full of hatred I almost did go crazy. All of it drained out of me when it dawned upon me that I had to stop thinking about all I had lost and start thinking about what I could gain, even from the worst of situations a person could be in. You are a source of strength to me . . . and I know that your mind wouldn't be hard-pressed enough to crack from an experience like this. To be wronged, as I've been, by an experience such as this, would be for you, as it is for me, an affront to your dignity, integrity and all else that you hold sacred, and you would know, as I do, that to crack would be to never be able to prove your innocence, and your mind would never allow itself to degenerate into a state where it couldn't strive to bring your innocence to the light and regain your freedom. Jan, I didn't harm or kill anyone and I can't allow myself to deteriorate to a state of being where I can no longer strive to prove my innocence.'

Sam's letters cover the gamut of human emotions. They reveal a man of great profundity, a man with the capacity for deep thought, and also a person with such a natural *joie de vivre* and love of laughter that even in the direst circumstances it bubbles through. For instance, Sam has laughingly taken it upon himself to teach Jan black American slang. Commenting on his progress he wrote: 'You are coming close to using "Main Man" like a "Brutha". (smile) Add "My" in front of "Main" and you will be "in there". (smile). "In there" is another term used by us meaning "on top of things". (smile). "Bro", I cracked my sides over Samuel 51 [Jan's last letter]. I can't help but laugh over how much "trash" you can talk. ha-ha-ha. Jan, you are SOMETHING ELSE! (smile) But, of course, I'm not telling you anything that you don't already know. ha-ha-ha. OKAY, "Mr Whittlesford Wonder". "The Parchman Pulverizer".'

Sam moves from the mundane to the profound with a natural ease. 'Let's both keep our great grins and chuckles going,' he writes, 'knowing that as the mystic, Julian of Norwich, said: "All will be well will be well will be well." Let's also trust in God, have faith in tomorrow and most of all believe in ourselves.'

Religious belief is a topic both Jan and Sam discuss with fervour. Jan has recently joined the Quaker movement. Sam, in his Death Row cell where a man's thoughts inevitably dwell on his own mortality, has had many years in which to develop his own religious philosophy. Many Death Row inmates turn to God in one form or another, especially those whose roots lie in the Deep South society which is steeped in religion and the teachings of the Old Testament. Sam was brought up as a Baptist but rejected the church as a young man. During his years on Death Row he has developed a very personal belief in God, a belief that is punctuated by doubts as he ponders the situation that he has found himself in. 'I strongly believe in God – or whatever name there is for Him,' he wrote to Jan, 'but I don't and can't accept the god these people [in prison] try to conceptualize and give to me.'

Searching for a creed that he can truly believe in, Sam has found himself, through Jan, in sympathy with the Quaker movement. In yet another of his many exchanges with Jan, he writes:

'I am not drawn towards fundamentalism, nor the Evangelical

Christian who sees everything in terms of Jesus. An absence of these things along with an absence of dogmas and Reverends is what makes the Friends so appealing to me. Friends, as I know them, allow one to experience "The Experience" instead of "Teaching" one the experience. There's a saying: "Do not follow in the footsteps of the Ancients, seek what they sought."

'Christianity, as I know it, won't allow one to do this but mandates that one follows directly in Christ's footsteps. Following directly in Christ's footsteps allows one to only experience what Christ did. I don't and can't say that this is wrong. I think and believe that there is MORE and I can only experience the MORE that I think and believe there is by being free of restrictions to feel it. My brother, you're a translator and in translating you interpret as you see and know things to be. Meanings vary as often as their interpretations as you know well. The Bible has been translated many times and who is to say that its meaning hasn't been changed during its translation? Man has the capability to do anything. We know that King James altered the Bible and we know too, that he wasn't filled with Divine Inspiration to re-write it. I believe in the Bible but there are things that I question in it as not being the Word of God but the word of man. Each day I am more attracted to the Quaker way of worship because the more I think about it, the more that it seems RIGHT. Love says it all. Love does it all. Love IS all. Loving FULLY is what it's all about and I KNOW that you know what I'm talking about even though I'm saying it pretty badly.'

The depth of the two men's friendship was tested about a year after the relationship began, when Jan decided, with Clive's assistance, to vist Sam in his Mississippi cell. The meeting of minds on paper is not always the same face to face. But for Sam and Jan the few hours that they were able to have together were a high point in both their lives. 'There was no strangeness at all,' says Jan. 'It was as if we had known each other all our lives,' Sam echoes his words. 'With Jan it was as though we had known each other eternally,' he says. 'We are so in tune with each other until there are no words for what we are to each other. Spiritual Brothers comes close but it doesn't competely define what we are to each other. Somewhere I have read that that which cannot be described has no end, and I think of us as being without end. We will always be.'

It is a relationship that both men find rewarding and enriching. From his prison cell, Sam, the man who seems to have nothing, reaches out and gives of his thoughts and emotions to his friend in England. Among the many passages from Sam's letters that are treasured by Jan, is the following:

'Sometimes it take losing something in order to find it and I think that our sufferings have enabled us to really find ourselves and appreciate ourselves in relation to life. From this experience I have been able to look at my life as that of sand in an hourglass, with each day being a grain of sand that filters through to the bottom. When all of the sand at the top filters through to the bottom my life won't really end but the hourglass will be turned over and my life will begin again with each grain of sand filtering though to the bottom identically as it filtered through before the hourglass was turned over and it's impossible for me to change any grain from falling as it fell before. I don't know if life is like this at all, but I do know that looking at life as being an experience that I will re-experience, unable to alter anything at all, makes me do all that I can to make this day and however many other days I have left within my hourglass, the best that I can, because this day is going to come to be again and, when it does, I won't be able to change anything about it, but only experience it again. As I've said, I don't really know if life is as I've tried to describe it or not but, if it is, and if I love all that I can this day, if I laugh all that I can this day, if I give all of the happiness that I can this day, if I do the least amount of bad that I can this day, then when this day comes back to me I won't want to change it even if I could.'

This is a man that the state of Mississippi wants to kill. His story, like Edward's, is unique. But it is one that is reflected in varying forms among many of the prisoners awaiting execution on Death Row. Most are not as eloquent or as strong as Sam. Many cannot even read or write. Sam speaks not only for himself but for the hundreds of others, both guilty and innocent, who await death at the hands of the state.

'The use of the death penalty is revenge,' says Sam, echoing the words of the Jackson minister, the Rev Colton Smith. 'They do not want to use that terminology but that is what it is. When a person can grow above feelings of revenge and forgive and not feel bitter, then they can become a whole person.' Writing to Jan about the death penalty, Sam says: 'Even though I am outnumbered and poor, I won't give up my fight to be free. The only weapons available to me are my words and I believe that I can bring this evil to light and show it for exactly what it is − Evil.'

Eleven

Of Death, Hate and Humanity

Well over 100 people have died in the execution chambers of the United States since the 1976 Supreme Court decision which effectively re-introduced capital punishment to the nation. There are approximately another 2,200 prisoners on Death Row awaiting the day they will be killed. If all these people were taken from their cells tomorrow, lined up in the Louisiana Superdome and shot, it would make headlines around the world as a massacre of overwhelming proportions. Taken one by one, their lives pass away almost unnoticed.

Assessing human life by numbers can be misleading. It is, for example, an interesting fact that these 2,200 condemned men and women account for only a small proportion of convicted murderers in the USA. There are 35,000 or so who are serving time for murder in the country's jails. Does this statistic make America more merciful or less so? It could be answered both ways. A question with a more revealing answer is: who are these 2,200 who have been singled out as deserving of the ultimate penalty? Why is Sam Johnson on Death Row and others not? Why did Edward Johnson die in the gas chamber? What is the common factor among the inmates of Death Row? Are they the most vicious, sadistic and vile killers the courts have had to deal with? Are they the Charles Mansons of the world? Are they terrorists? Clive Stafford Smith says not.

Poverty is without doubt the greatest bond these condemned men and women have in common with each other, he says. Those on Death Row are, almost without exception, poor and unable to afford to pay for good legal representation. 'We have a saying in this country,' says Clive. 'We say we call it capital punishment because those with the capital don't get the punishment.' His words are reinforced by a fellow campaigner against the death penalty. 'You won't find the rich, white, privileged of this world

145

on Death Row,' says Joe Ingle. 'They never come close.' A man or woman charged with murder in the United States, who cannot afford the fees of private attorneys, is usually provided with a court-appointed or legal-aid lawyer. Most American attorneys are unwilling to take on such cases as the work load is high and the fee is low. 'The only time you get a good private attorney taking on a murder case where the person can't afford to pay, is if it is such a sensational case there will be a lot of publicity,' says Clive. In a recent murder trial he handled he was paid 51 cents an hour. 'That is the price the US puts on life,' he says. In order to bring the message home he is suing the state for failing to pay the minimum wage of well over $3 an hour stipulated by the Federal Government.

As a result of the poor remuneration, murder cases are all too often handled by recently qualified, inexperienced or even incompetent lawyers. 'I know of one murder case where the guy's attorney was still a student,' says Clive. 'There is another one where the guy's lawyer had never been in court before.' The situation becomes even worse after conviction. At that point most states do not provide any financial help for the prisoner at all. He has a right to appeal against his sentence and conviction but in order to do so he must rely on help from lawyers like Clive, lawyers who work for charitably funded organisations such as the Southern Prisoners' Defence Committee which will ask no fee. Otherwise he must try to handle the legal process himself. The number of lawyers prepared to forego the large salaries available to attorneys in private practice in America is very limited. There are far too few lawyers like Clive who are prepared to sacrifice material rewards for the sake of an ideal. Many prisoners have to resort to trying to present their own appeals with the help of the access they are given to the prison law library.

A condemned man on Death Row in Virginia has given an eloquent description of the plight of some of his fellow prisoners, many of whom are poorly educated, some of whom are mentally retarded. 'Let me ask you to picture yourself in this situation,' writes Joe Giarratano in an anti-death penalty newsletter.

'You've been convicted of capital murder and sentenced to death. You are indigent, functionally illiterate and mildly retarded. Your court-appointed trial lawyer tells you that you have the right to appeal [against] your conviction and sentence, but that he will no longer represent you.

'He tells you that you must either hire an attorney or represent yourself . . . . An execution date is set and you have only 30 days to do something. You have no money to hire a lawyer, you cannot find one who will represent you free, the judge who set your execution date refuses to appoint counsel to assist you and you've been moved into the death house. Your only choice is for you to represent yourself.

'You must file something with the court or be executed in less than 30 days .... But before you can file you must learn to read, write, over- come your retardation, obtain your trial transcript, understand the science of law, learn how to conduct legal research, analyse vast amounts of case law, formulate your issues, learn all the procedures, learn all the various court rules, understand civil procedure, constitutional law, criminal law and acquire the art of legal writing .... I may be wrong but it appears to me that your right to appeal, under the outlined circum- stances, is nothing more than a meaningless and empty abstraction.'

Socio-economic class is one of two major factors that will lead a convicted murderer to Death Row. The colour of a man's skin is the other. According to Amnesty International, the worldwide, independent organisation which seeks to protect human rights, blacks account for 12 per cent of the population of the United States but more than 40 per cent of those currently on Death Row. This inconsistency can be partly accounted for by the fact that, in the Southern states especially, being poor and being black often go hand in hand.

But it is not simply the colour of the skin of the man awaiting execution that tips the scales against black people. The colour of the victim is equally important. In November 1988, of all the prisoners on Death Row, only 43 white people had been sentenced to death for killing blacks, whereas 727 black people were awaiting execution for killing whites. Taking into account the fact that half of all those arrested for murder are black, what the statistics seem to say is if you are black and kill a white person, you are more likely to be executed than a white who kills a black person. It has been argued that this discrepancy can be explained by the fact that since blacks are more commonly poor and unemployed, they more often kill white people during the course of robbery or theft, thus making it a capital murder charge. But studies conducted among prisoners on Death Row show this is a flawed argument. One investigation of prisoners on Florida Death Row showed, for example, that 47 per cent of blacks and only 24 per cent of whites arrested for murdering whites in felony circumstances ended up on Death Row. It is also significant that, as yet, no white convicted of the single murder of a black has in fact gone to the exeuction chamber.

The difference between execution and life imprisonment is also dictated by which part of the United States a person comes from. Of the 50 states in the Union, 36 have the death penalty on their statute books. Not all make use of it. The great stronghold of capital punishment lies in the Southern states. More than half of all Death Row inmates are incarcerated in the Deep South. Texas, Florida and Louisiana lead the league table in the numbers of people executed. It is here that support for the death penalty is at its strongest. It is here that Clive Stafford Smith and his colleagues concentrate their efforts.

They are not totally alone in their battle. There are many people in the United States who support them, but they are still a minority of the population. There are thousands of people throughout the world who have joined the campaign against capital punishment anywhere, people who are backing Amnesty International in its fight against the death penalty. In one small corner of England, as a result of Jan Arriens' initiative alone, there are scores of people demonstrating their abhorrence of legalised state killing. After learning of Jan's action and relationship with Sam Johnson through articles in Jan's local paper, the *Cambridge Weekly News*, and the Quaker magazine, *The Friend*, they have followed his example and are writing to prisoners on Death Row in America. A loosely knit group of about 150 people has grown up with Jan at its centre. They come from all walks of life and all age groups, ranging from an 80-year-old man to a 15-year-old schoolgirl. Some of them, like Jan, have developed close relationships with the people they are writing to. With others the correspondence is more sporadic. Many of the prisoners, unlike Sam Johnson, are barely literate. They respond as best they can. This is a section from a letter from one such prisoner in Alabama. 'I really appreciate you taking time to write an say hello,' he writes. 'I thank god for sending me a friend, I hope we can correspond regular, it will give me something to look forward to. There is nothing to do in here but write an hope peoples will write back, I have been praying for a friend to write, an maybe you are the answer to my prayers.'

The English letter writers fill a vital role, holding out the hand of friendship and support to Death Row inmates who often have little or no contact with the outside world, and little to live for. Sam Johnson spoke for many when he described how he felt when he received his first letter from Jan. 'I was totally overwhelmed seeing the mailman stop with a letter addressed to me. Not addressed to 'Occupant'. A real letter. Addressed to me! Me, a black man in a white society, a person who this society has judged not worthy of life. I've received a real letter. One letter turns into several. Several give life to a friend I've never met. Thoughts, real thoughts are exchanged. The darkness that is my world diminishes.' Jan's list of those who would like to write grows every day.

There are also some among the born and bred Southerners of the United States who feel as strongly opposed to the death penalty as Clive. One such is a 43-year-old ordained minister by the name of Joe Ingle. Based in Nashville, Tennessee, he runs an organisation called the Southern Coalition on Jails and Prisons, which has offices throughout the Deep South. He is a minister without a church. His parishioners are the men and women in prison, especially those on Death Row. He spends his time campaigning against the death penalty, working with those on Death Row, visiting their families, and talking to numerous groups and organisations throughout the Southern states and the rest of the world in an attempt to make people aware of the full horror and barbarity of what state execution really means. He has great respect for the work undertaken by Clive and the other lawyers working for the Southern Prisoners' Defence Committee. 'They have literally saved lives,' he says. 'What they have done is remarkable on very little money.' In 1989, as in the previous year, Joe Ingle was nominated to receive the Nobel Peace Prize for his work. He says of the nomination: 'The sad reality is that it is an expression of our Western European allies' growing outrage that the US alone remains in league with South Africa, the USSR and countries like Iran in our persistent use of the death penalty.'

A story of Joe Ingle's helps to explain his own motivation for the work he does and, he hopes, demonstrates to his fellow countrymen that he is more than just a conscience-stricken priest with liberal beliefs. Joe Ingle is a Southerner, born and raised in North Carolina. He knows the way his people feel. When a young man still studying at a seminary in New York, he decided that he would like to find out more about prisoners and their conditions. He therefore arranged to become a regular visitor at a large detention centre in the Bronx.

'I can remember just like it was yesterday the first time I went into that place.... The guard led me round and showed me to a small room and said it was where people usually visited. I looked at that and, being a naïve student, I looked over at the large cage with its individual cells where the prisoners were housed and said: "Why don't you let me in there with those men?" The guard looked at me like "It's your life", shrugged and opened the barred door and I stepped in. All the individual cells were open. In the first one a guy was sitting on his bunk. As soon as I stepped through the barred door, the guard slammed it shut behind me. I can still feel that because what went through my mind instantaneously with the slamming of that door was: "Oh, my God, they have locked me in here with these animals."

'Just as I had thought that, this guy sitting in the first cell looked up and said: "Man, what are you doing here?" I laughed and said: "Well, I'm here to visit you guys." He said sit down, so I did and he introduced himself and then he took me down and introduced me to everyone on that side of the cell block. And I always remember that because that was the way I was socialised, to regard people in jail as less than human. That's the way we are all socialised in this country.

'When I talk about it in front of groups I tell them this story so they will understand I had the same feelings as them. I spent the year visiting those guys and it was just a real experience. Everyone I visited was either black or Puerto Rican except one white guy. No-one had been convicted, they were all awaiting trial. They were there because they were poor and could not afford bail. So I really saw for the first time the way the American system of so-called justice works. They were poor, they were coloured and they were basically the kind of folks that American society does not care or want to worry about. That year I learned so much. It taught me so much about what my country was doing to people who we regard as different from us.'

Together with three others, a methodist minister, a Catholic priest and a lawyer, Joe Ingle went on to found the Southern Coalition on Jails and Prisons in 1974. With the US Supreme Court decision in 1976 which unlocked the doors of the execution chambers after a moratorium of several years, and precipitated the acceleration of legalised killing which continues today, the organisation began to concentrate its efforts on working for the abolition of capital punishment. 'What we are doing in this country with 2,200 people on Death Row is just an extension of what I found out in the Bronx House of Detention,' Joe Ingle believes. 'Once you start regarding people in jail as less than human, once you start that psychological process of dehumanising someone, it is very hard to stop it. And that's what leads you to the death house. You are able to treat people in horrendous ways because you see them as sub-human. I really feel that my role in all this is to help people understand what we are doing in this country. I go out and talk to ordinary people, the people I grew up with. They do not see the humanness of people on Death Row. All they see is a little blurb in the newspaper and, by and large, they have never seen anyone in prison let alone on Death Row. So people have these stereotype images.'

One such man who at first glance would seem to fit the image perfectly was Leo Edwards. He was executed in June 1989, having lost his final appeal against his death sentence. Leo was black and had been on Mississippi Death Row since 1981, convicted of robbing and murdering three white men during several days of crime which terrorised the residents of Jackson, Mississippi. Leo Edwards had a long criminal record for robbery. At the time the killings took place he was an escaped prisoner on the run. He was a regular drug user. There are a great many people throughout the world who would say that Leo Edwards was a menace to society and deserved to die. Three innocent people lost their lives because of his action. Three families have been devastated by the terrible tragedy of losing their loved ones suddenly and violently. Locking this villain up and throwing away the key would have been too good for him.

But those who knew and met Leo during his last few years while he was a prisoner at Parchman Penitentiary found it hard to visualise the man sitting on the other side of the barred divide as a homicidal drug-crazed maniac. He was a quiet, reserved, excessively polite man with a sensitive and gentle face. He talked haltingly in a sad low voice. He was like a maltreated pet animal, which responds to any kindness or friendship, but is ready to turn and run at the first sign of hostility or rejection. He was a pitiable, but not pitiful figure. 'I liked Leo,' says Clive. He represented him for many years and, as with Edward, fought almost until the final hour to save him. 'He was just the nicest, most thoughtful person around.'

Many of those who know Leo's life story do not find it hard to understand where and why it went wrong. Like so many other Death Row prisoners, he came from a poor, deprived background. His family life was unhappy, and he was the victim of abuse from his alcoholic father. He grew up in New Orleans knowing little of love and family warmth. As a young man, poorly educated and lacking the skills to obtain work, he turned to petty theft. While in prison he was introduced to drugs, thus he became part of the vicious cycle of drugs, crime and prison.

The prison authorities make no attempt to rehabilitate or educate those who end up on Death Row. There seems little point to them in doing anything to help a person the state intends to kill. This policy runs all the way down the line, even into the dental surgery where if a condemned man has a decayed tooth, it is extracted rather than filled. It explains why so many men on Death Row have missing teeth.

But despite the lack of any assistance or, until the last few months, encouragement, Leo Edwards managed to make something of his life on Death Row. Simply through his use of the prison library, he gave himself a little of the education he never had as a child. For the last year of his life he had a regular correspondence with a Cambridge woman who contacted him through Jan Arriens. Suzanne O'Callaghan never met Leo, but feels she knew him well through his letters. 'I found him very perceptive and intelligent,' she says. 'I would describe him as quiet, gentle, sensitive and very reflective. I saw him as a man with tremendous gifts and potential which he never had the opportunity to develop. Leo was anything but a violent, hardened criminal.'

Clive would agree. 'What Leo illustrated,' he said, 'is that education can change people who have not had the opportunity to be educated. It is a fairly weird form of education to put someone on Death Row and tell them for ten years that you are going to kill them, although it has been effective with some of these guys. But there are things other than condemning a man to die that could be done, which would be just as effective for someone who is on drugs and does not have the wherewithal for a normal decent life. That is where America fails in providing the habilitation in the first place. They do nothing for people in prison so that is why, with someone like Leo who was in prison, they come out worse than before. He had been getting drugs in prison. They had done nothing to help him straighten out his life. He couldn't get a job because he was an ex-con. He couldn't get welfare because there is no such thing as welfare. So what was he meant to do? He had two choices. He either starved or he went back to his old ways. The sad thing is that, like Leo, there are quite a few people on Death Row who are very intelligent, very articulate. They are people who have potential.'

For Leo, though, it is too late. He died in the gas chamber at Parchman Penitentiary on June 21st, 1989. Talking about his impending fate to a prison chaplain, he said: 'He asked me what did I feel and how would I like to be remembered. I told him I would like to be forgotten. When I said that, I felt like that was how I've always felt. Like no-one loves me so no-one should remember me.'

On June 17th Leo wrote a letter of farewell to Suzanne O'Callaghan in England. 'I am at a great loss of words on this occasion because your friendship and concern has really made my heart smile with the life you've brought it, and it's extremely difficult to say goodbye to you but I must ...' wrote Leo. 'I leave this life with nothing as I came into it. But I hurt for those whom my death will hurt, their pain is what I feel and fear most ... Death will put an end to all my lovelessness, emptiness, heartache and pain so I am grateful for that . . . It's very ironic that one must face death to know life: since I've been here I've come to know and feel every aspect of life and love, only to die before I can share it.'

Clive fought long and hard for Leo, and is deeply saddened to have failed. He is also angered by the reasons for his failure, which he sees as yet another example of the 'heads we win, tails you lose' attitude of the American judicial system. In 1986, in a case concerning a prisoner in Kentucky, the US Supreme Court ruled that it was unconstitutional for a prosecutor to strike black people from a jury because of the colour of their skin. As a result of that ruling, another of Clive's clients has had his conviction for murder overturned and a re-trial ordered. That man, Willie Gamble, is black and had been convicted by an all-white jury in Georgia. Leo Edwards was black. He too was convicted by an all-white jury. The prosecuting District Attorney in Leo's case is even on record as saying at the time that he did not think that black people should be allowed to serve on juries as they had no sense of justice. Leo had argued since 1982 that the racial make-up of his jury was unconstitutional, but, despite the 1986 Supreme Court decision, the courts refused to concede the point in his case. For that decision was not retroactive; its ruling does not apply to cases heard before 1986. So Clive's Georgia client Willie, whose case started a few weeks after the ruling, won his appeal and Leo did not, although the grounds were the same.

In the last week of Leo's life, Clive asked the US Supreme Court to grant a stay of execution. It refused. He appealed to the Governor of Mississippi for clemency. Governor Ray Mabus turned him down saying racial discrimination had no bearing on the case. The day that Leo died, the Governor spoke at a meeting to commemorate the 25th anniversary of the murder of the three civil rights workers in Philadelphia, Mississippi, a meeting which was held to demonstrate that Mississippi had come to terms with its racist past and that the three young men had not died in vain. Governor Mabus saw no conflict between giving his support to this meeting and on the same day sanctioning the death of a black man who had been condemned by a jury which had demonstrated the continuing existence of racial prejudice within the judicial system.

'Although Leo argued all along that he was the victim of racial prejudice, he lost. Willie won because his case started ten days after the Kentucky decision,' says Clive bitterly. 'That is the difference between life and death. For Leo it was just fundamentally unfair. The reason they say the ruling of the US Supreme Court is not retroactive is because the prosecutors were not under notice of it at the time. Who cares whether they were on notice or not? Here they were, intentionally discriminating. It may not have been the law at the time but everyone knows you don't go striking black people from juries just because of the colour of their faces. It is outrageous, absolutely disgusting.'

Unfairness in relation to the death penalty is not a concept that carries much weight in America. Joe Ingle knows that too. 'We in this country have a mean streak,' he says. 'Even if we find evidence of innocence it does not necessarily affect the death penalty. We would say: "So, we have made a mistake but look at all the other ones who deserve it." That is how cold we are. Life is cheap, especially black life.'

He argues that, contrary to popular belief, the death penalty is not a deterrent to murder. American universities have studied the correlation between homicides and capital punishment and published figures that show that execution does not reduce the number of murders taking place. 'States that execute criminals don't necessarily enjoy lower homicide rates than states that don't use the death penalty,' says Joe Ingle. 'If anything, capital punishment encourages more murder by institutionalising it in the name of the state, by seeming to enshrine a disregard for human life in the codes of government. I respect people who are honest about their position on the death penalty when they say they simply want revenge. That's the only understandable reason you can be in favour of capital punishment. It's not a deterrent, it has no social value, it's costly, it's inhumane, it's arbitrary and it's inequitably applied. But if you just say: "Hey, I want revenge," I can at least relate to that at the gut level. I come from a family of redneck white Southerners. But let's call it what it is − bloodlust.'

What does state execution achieve for the vast mass of people? The answer, according to another American minister, is summed up in one word: 'Nothing'. Henry Hudson, the priest in charge of St Paul's Episcopalian Church in Meridian, Mississippi, knows that from personal experience. He reluctantly witnessed the first execution to take place at Parchman Penitentiary after the 1976 Supreme Court ruling. He had been asked to do so by the man destined to die, who wanted someone close by who loved him. Henry Hudson was able to give that Christian love. 'People came to witness that execution full of hate,' he says. 'They gathered outside the prison and they were full of hate. They thought that by executing this man suddenly something was going to happen and the hate would be removed. But nothing happened, nothing at all. They were still full of hate but then it was worse because they had killed a man. Nothing had been achieved but another life had been taken.' That execution took place several years ago but it remains a vivid memory in Henry Hudson's mind. It is an event he will never get over. Each year when the anniversary of the execution comes round, he retreats into himself and for several weeks is a pale image of his real self.

Hate and revenge. Those are the two words that are repeated time and time again in conversations about the use of the death penalty in the USA. They are the words used by one woman, who knows from the depth of her soul what it is like to feel such hate and revenge. Dorothea Moorfield is a middle-aged mother from Washington DC. Her son was murdered, shot repeatedly in cold blood at the age of nineteen. He and four others were killed in a fast food restaurant where he worked in the evenings to help finance his college education. Dorothea Moorfield had never given much thought to the use of the death penalty until that terrible day when her son died. Now she spends her time campaigning against capital punishment. In 1989, together with Clive Stafford Smith, she spoke at an Amnesty International meeting in London held as part of the organisation's year-long campaign against the use of the death penalty throughout the world. This is what she had to say:

'I was devastated by the death of my son. I could not begin to understand what had happened. My pain turned to rage against the killer and I hated him. I wanted him to die, to die slowly and painfully. I would have killed him myself. I said I wanted justice. But what I wanted was revenge. This feeling was destroying me. I had to work my way through this hatred. If you stop at hate you are going to be destroyed too. Gradually I realised that what I wanted was not a life for a life. It was another death. It was more violence. It took a long time but I chose to put it aside. What I am campaigning for now, what I am arguing for throughout the world, is a respect for the sanctity of all lives.'

That, too, is what Clive Stafford Smith works towards. That is the belief that gives him the strength and motivation to continue despite the constant setbacks, the judicial injustices and the personal pain and sadness that he experiences. That is why he still continues to battle for Edward Johnson, whose story of life and death illustrates so much that Clive believes is wrong within the United States. When and if the death penalty is abolished in America, Clive will know that Edward did not die in vain. It is an issue, he says, of humanity.

Appendix

Saying NO to the death penalty

When the state kills ...

In the past decade literally thousands of people have been executed in scores of countries around the world. Men, women and even children have been hanged, shot dead, electrocuted, gassed, poisoned, beheaded or stoned to death as a result of judicial orders.

Many of the executed were convicted of brutal crimes. Others died for non-violent offences, including 'economic corruption' and adultery. Many went to their deaths for purely political reasons or after blatantly unfair trials. Some were prisoners of conscience. Nobody knows the exact number of innocent victims of execution. Cruel, arbitrary and irrevocable, the death penalty is imposed disproportionately on the poor and powerless. It is a violation of human rights.

A world without executions?

Already 80 countries in the world no longer use the death penalty. Most Western European countries have abolished it, and in 1987 the German Democratic Republic became the first East European nation to do so. The United Nations is actively promoting worldwide abolition.

But some 100 countries still retain the death penalty. In the United States, 36 of the 51 states currently permit capital punishment. At present there are over 2,000 men, women and juveniles (people under 18 at the time of the crime) awaiting execution. The challenge is to persuade all these countries to join the growing band of abolitionist countries – to make a world without executions.

157

Amnesty International's anti-death penalty campaign

Amnesty International is a worldwide movement which seeks the release of prisoners of conscience, opposes the death penalty, torture and other cruel, inhuman or degrading treatment or punishment for prisoners, and advocates fair and early trial for all political prisoners.

Amnesty International's anti-death penalty campaign is challenging the presence and use of the death penalty throughout the world. In addition, the campaign is focussing on the seven countries that between them execute the majority of the people killed as a result of the imposition of the judicial death penalty. These countries are: USA, USSR, China, Iran, Iraq, South Africa and Nigeria.

Amnesty International is calling on all countries to stop executions immediately and permanently; commute all outstanding death sentences; abolish the death penalty in law. It is publicising objections to the death penalty in the countries concerned, promoting and discussing Amnesty's opposition with local organisations, and promoting debate in the national media and amongst politicians and the legal, medical and other professions.

You can help!

Worldwide abolition will become a reality when people like you throughout the world say NO to the death penalty. Join Amnesty International's international campaign against the death penalty and say YES to a world without executions.

For more information contact Amnesty International:

Australia	PO Box A159, Sydney South, New South Wales 2000 (Tel: 2 267 2075)
Austria	Wiedner Guertel 12/7, A-1040 Wien (Tel: 222 405 4320)
Barbados	PO Box 872, Bridgetown (Tel: 809 428 9331)
Belgium	(Flemish) Kerkstraat 156, 2008 Antwerpen (Tel: 3 271 1616)
	(French speaking) 9 Rue Berckmans, 1060 Bruxelles (Tel: 2 538 8175/77)

Canada	(English speaking) 130 Slater Street, Suite 900, Ottawa, Ontario, K1P 6E2 (Tel: 613 563 1891)
	(French speaking) 3516 Ave du Parc, Montreal, Quebec H2X 2117 (Tel: 514 288 1141)
Denmark	Frederiksborggade 1, 1360 Copenhagen K (Tel: 1 117541)
Finland	Ruoholahdenkatu 24, SF-00180, Helsinki (Tel: 0 6931 488/975/928)
France	4 Rue de la Pierre Levee, 75553 Paris (Cedex 11) (Tel: 143 387474)
Germany, Federal Republic of	Heerstrasse 178, 5300 Bonn 1 (Tel: 228 650981)
Greece	20 Mavromihali Street, Athens 106–80 (Tel: 1 360 0628)
Hong Kong	216 Beverley Commercial Centre, 87–105 Chatham Road, Kowloon (Tel: 3 722 1872)
Iceland	PO Box 618, 121 Reykjavik (Tel: 1 16940)
India	c/o Dateline Delhi, 21 North End Complex, Panchkuin Road, New Delhi 10001 (Tel: 11 310799)
Ireland	8 Shaw Street, Dublin 2 (Tel: 1 776361)
Italy	viale Mazzini 146, 00195 Rome (Tel: 6 380898/ 389403)
Japan	Daisan-Sanbu Building 3F, 2–3–22 Nishi-Waseda, Shinjuku-ku, Tokyo (Tel: 3 2031050)
Luxembourg	Boite Postale 1914, 1019 Luxembourg (Tel: 481687)
Netherlands	Keizersgracht 620, 1017 ER Amsterdam (Tel: 20 264436)
New Zealand	PO Box 6647, Te Aro, Wellington 1 (Tel: 4 849774)
Norway	Maridalsveien 87, 0461 Oslo 4 (Tel: 2 380032)
Portugal	Apartado 1642, 1016 Lisboa Codex (Tel: 1 523537)
Spain	Paseo de Recoletos 18, Piso 6, 28001 Madrid (Tel: 1 275 4118)
Sweden	Gyllenstiernsgatan 18, S-115 26 Stockholm (Tel: 8 663 1900)

Switzerland	PO Box 1051, CH – 3001 Bern (Tel: 31 257966)
Trinidad and Tobago	PO Bag 231, Woodbrook PO, Port of Spain, Trinidad (Tel: 627 6050)
United Kingdom	99–119 Rosebery Avenue, London EC1R 4RE (Tel: 1 278 6000)
USA	322 8th Avenue, New York, NY 10001 (Tel: 212 807 8400)